师宴客

# BONG LAM

## A COOKBOOK

### FOR

## POPULAR CHINESE FOOD

*Bong Lam.*

Author: **Kin Bong Lam**
Executive Producer: **Dorian Chan**
Design & Art Director: **Xunbo Tang**
Photographer: **Xunbo Tang**
Food Stylists: **Kin Bong Lam, Andy Lau**
Graphic Page Layout: **Colourcraft Studio Ltd.**
Editor: **Kathy Cheng**

First published in Great Britain in 2012 by M8 Consultants (GB) Limited.
31 Bullock Street, Birmingham B7 4DY United Kingdom. Website: www.m8gb.com

Copyright © M8 Consultants (GB) Limited 2012

ISBN 978-0-9573452-0-1
Printed and bound in China

Publisher's note
Although the advice and information in this book are believed to be accurate and true at the time of going to press,
neither the authors nor the publisher can accept any legal responsibility or liability for any errors or omissions that may have been made
nor for any inaccuracies nor for any loss, harm or injury that comes about from following instructions or advice in this book.

# CONTENTS

# Foreword

Chinese cuisine is widely seen as representing one of the richest and most diverse culinary heritages in the world. It originated in the many varied regions of China and has been introduced to other parts of the world, from Southeast Asia to North America and Western Europe.

If cooking is an art, Chinese cooking enriches it with unlimited scope for creative flair and a stylistic touch. Great attention is paid to the presentation of the food. A good Chinese dish should whet the appetite with its appearance and luxuriant aromas - piping hot steam as the dim sum basket is opened, or the tang of the spices from the aromatic crispy duck - before delighting the tongue.

Shopping daily for fresh ingredients is essential for all Chinese cooking, whether it is live seafood, fresh meats, seasonal fruits or vegetables from the local market. Swimming fish, snapping crabs, and clucking chickens ensure the freshest produced!

However, many Chinese dishes are easy to cook; fried rice with egg for example, takes only minutes to make. Others, such as "Jiiaozi" (or stuffed dumpling with leek and pork), noodles, sweet and sour spare ribs, may take longer but still require only a few simple steps. Many of the ingredients are readily available at the local supermarket, while others may require a trip to a Chinese or Asian market or the use of an appropriate substitute.

This book contains a selection of over 100 Chinese recipes, shown in more than 200 stunning photographs. Each is simple to follow and quick to prepare without compromising on taste. Everything from appetizers to desserts, soups or dim sum and sauces, including some of my iconic creations, epitomizing my unique interpretation of Chinese cuisine.

As a Chinese cuisine lover, I am constantly exploring new ways to create more memorable and great tasting dishes. My greatest delight is in hearing of my readers' triumphs in preparing the dishes from this book.

# About the Author

Bong Lam was born in Zhuhai city, Guangdong province of China. At 15, he moved from China to Macau, where he started his apprenticeship at a Chinese restaurant learning to become a chef. Started from the bottom, Bong's duty was varies from pushing dim sum trolley at the restaurant floor to washing vegetables in the kitchen.

In 1980, Bong Lam moved to Hong Kong, brought with him only what he had learnt from his apprenticeship, he got a job as a dim sum chef in a district restaurant. After mastering his craft, Bong Lam was appointed by a 5 star Hong Kong hotel restaurant, to work as their head dim sum chef at the tourist district of Tsim Sha Tsui, Hong Kong.

A new employment opportunity offer from a famous restautant group in UK gave Bong Lam his opportunity to work in London Chinatown from 1992 to 1997. One of the restaurant's regular customer, Mr W Wing Yip, was so captivated by his dim sum skill, and persuaded him to open Bong Lam's first restaurant Wing Wah in Birmingham.

The next 15 years, Bong Lam founded Wing Wah Group, of which he is the chairman. Today, the group has grown to a multifaceted enterprise. Apart from 7 restaurants based in West Midlands, a trendy patisserie, a food factory, a consultancy company specialise in restaurant contracting work.

In 2011, Bong Lam was awarded Master Chef by World Association of Chinese Cuisine, the highest honour in Chinese cuisine worldwide.

Bong Lam established his Educational Bursary in 2011 to encourage UK Chinese children to learn Chinese language in China. The famous Jinan University in Guangdong province is one of the universities in China offers schemes to accept overseas Chinese to study in China. Bong Lam's educational Bursary enable many fulfilling their dreams.

Sharing his culinary skill is one of Bong Lam's contribution to his fellow chefs. In this cookbook, he has given us the insight of how traditional Chinese foods should be prepared, and the origin of many dishes. He believes every mouthful of food, has a link in Chinese history. From centuries history evolved to modern dining, there is no short cut in cooking good Chinese food.

Cooking is a labour of love, with his love of cooking, Bong Lam wishes everyone who uses his recipes will enjoy as much as he does.

# Honors and Awards

**International Master Chef**
for Chinese Cuisine
by World Association of Chinese Cuisine

**BRITISH CULINARY
FEDERATION**
National Member of the World
Association of Chefs' Societies

**Master Chef**
World Association of Chinese Cuisine

**Member**

| | |
|---|---|
| **Chairman** | Wing Wah Group, UK |
| **President** | Confederation of Chinese Business (UK) |
| **President** | Zhuhai Co-operative Association (UK) |
| **Member** | Zhuhai Chinese Cuisine Association |
| **Honorary President** | Confederation of Chinese Associations UK |
| **Honorary President** | UK Chinese Education Foundation |
| **President** | Bong Lam Educational Bursary |
| **Non-Executive Governer** | Birmingham Chinese School |
| **Non-Executive Governor** | Overseas Chinese Association School |

# Culture

Cuisines

Symbolism

Manners

# Cuisines

There are varieties of Chinese food cover all over China as the large territory. Generally speaking, it is widely accepted that Chinese food can be divided into eight regional cuisines.

## Shandong Cuisine

One of the oldest major cuisines in China, Shandong cuisine emphasises aroma, freshness, crispness and tenderness, and focuses on roasting, stir-frying, and deep-frying. Shandong cuisine often uses shallot and garlic as seasonings. The most famous dish of Shandong cuisine is the Sweet and Sour Carp.

## Szechuan Cuisine

Szechuan is one of the most famous Chinese cuisines in the world, known especially for using dried bird's-eye chillies and Szechuan peppercorns to produce the distinctive spicy and numb taste sensations. The main Szechuan cooking techniques are stir-frying, pickling and braising.

## Canton Cuisine

Probably the richest cuisine in China, Cantonese cuisine is especially popular in western countries. Almost all the cooking techniques are used, though stir-frying and steaming in particular are commonly applied. It places great emphasis on bringing out the natural flavour of the ingredients, although artistic presentation of the dishes is also highly emphasised by the Canton chef.

## Fujian Cuisine

Perhaps unsurprisingly, due to its coastal location, Fujian is most famous for seafood dishes. It is especially popular for the distinctive choices of seafood that focus on the colour of the dish. It emphasises sweet, sour and salty flavours, for which its characteristic marinades are commonly used.

### Jiangsu Cuisine

Jiangsu Cuisine focuses on the freshness of the ingredients, which is one of the reasons for its trademark light and sweet flavour. Stewing, braising and roasting are the commonly used cooking techniques, though Jiangsu cuisine is also well known for carving techniques, especially melon carving.

### Zhejiang Cuisine

Popular local cuisines from Hangzhou, Shaoxing and Ningbo make up Zhejiang cuisine. Here the emphasis is on exploiting the freshness, tenderness, softness and smoothness of the ingredients.

### Hunan cuisine

Most people think of Hunan cuisine as being rather similar to Szechuan cuisine since they are both spicy. Actually, the spiciness of Hunan cuisine is more pungent than numbing: chillies, peppers and shallots are necessary ingredients.

### Anhui Cuisine

Anhui cuisine focuses on the temperature during the process of cooking, and stewing is the preferred cooking method. Additions, such as ham and rock sugar, are used to enhance the flavour of the dishes.

# Symbolism

In China, foods are given particular meanings and food also is an important part of daily life. The Chinese not only enjoy eating, but believe eating good food can bring harmony and closeness to the family and other relationships. So, food has a special meaning to the Chinese people.

For instance, noodles are the symbol of longevity in Chinese culture. They are as much a part of a Chinese birthday celebration as a birthday cake with lit candles is in many countries, so that youngsters and seniors all will have a bowl of Long Life Noodles in the expectation of a healthy life. Since noodles do symbolize long life, it is considered very unlucky to cut up a strand.

Eggs hold a special symbolic significance in many cultures, and China is no exception. The Chinese believe eggs symbolize fertility. After a baby is born, parents may hold a "red egg and ginger party", where they serve round hard-boiled eggs to announce the birth.

Ducks represent fidelity in Chinese culture. If you are ever invited to a Chinese wedding banquet, don't be surprised to see a mouth-watering platter of Peking duck on the banquet table. Also, red dishes are common at weddings, as red is the colour of happiness.

Fish also play a large role in festive celebrations. The Chinese word for fish "Yu" sounds like the Chinese words for both wish and abundance. As a result, on New Year's Eve it is customary to serve a fish for dinner, symbolizing the wish for prosperity and wealth in the coming year. In addition, the fish is served whole, with head and tail attached, symbolizing a good beginning and ending for the coming year.

Chicken forms part of the symbolism of the dragon and phoenix in Chinese culture. At a Chinese wedding, chicken's feet, referred to as phoenix feet, are often served with dragon foods such as lobster. Chicken is also popular at Chinese New Year, symbolizing a good marriage and the coming together of families, and serving the bird whole emphasizes family unity.

Seeds, such as lotus seeds and watermelon seeds, represent the bearing of many children in Chinese culture. Visit an Asian bakery during the Chinese New Year, and you're likely to find a plethora of snacks with different types of seeds in them. There are other foods, snacks and fruits which symbolize good wishes under special circumstances, including dried bean curd, black moss seaweed, peanuts, pomelos and oranges.

# Manners

In China, eating is a very important part of the culture, rather similar to the drinking with friends in a bar in the west. It is a way to maintain and deepen friendships and to show hospitality when socialising with guests.

## Seating

Seating arrangements are important in Chinese dining. Normally, the most important people, such as elders or invited guests, would be given the best seats, as a mark of respect. Commonly, this would be against the back wall of the room, facing the main door. Others, according to their status or age, to sit from inside to outside.

## Inviting Guests

Showing respect to the guests is always the priority in the Chinese dining:

The host would stand up to welcome when the guests arrived, then sit down until the guest is seated. Then the host would be responsible for ordering the dish.

The meal always starts with a toast from the host. In return, the guest should make a toast to the host in the middle of the meal.

The host should invite the guest to start the meal first. As a way of showing respect, it is common for the host to us his or her chopsticks to serve the guest some food.

Guests should not "split the bill" with the host as it will make the host very embarrassing. However, the guest could offer a meal to invite the host in return next time.

## Using Chopsticks

Never use the chopsticks with different length.

Chopsticks must be put neatly and tidily on the table when not being used.

Do not point at others or wave around with your chopsticks.

Never stick chopsticks in a bowl of rice as it represents burning the incense in the funeral.

Do not tap the plate or bowl with the chopsticks as this is considered very impolite.

## Using Teapot

Do not point the spout of the teapot at anyone as it means that person is not welcome. Make it outward from the table.

When pouring tea to others, you should use your right hand to hold the teapot and use the left hand to keep the lid in place.

When other is pouring tea for you, you should use the knuckles of the first and middle fingers to tap the table two to three times to show your appreciation.

# Cooking Techniques

## Stir-frying

The most widely used Chinese cooking technique is stir-frying. It allows foods to be cooked with little oil in a short time, allowing the nutrition, natural flavours and textures of the foods to be retained.

When stir-frying it is important to prepare all the required ingredients in advance, since once cooking starts there will be no time for chopping.

To start, heat the wok or frying pan on a high heat, then swirl the oil around its surface. The oil can be flavoured with chopped spring onions, garlic or ginger, but do not heat the oil until it smokes as those seasonings will be quickly burnt.

Next, add the prepared ingredients required by the recipe, but remember to dry them before adding, or the oil will spit. If there is too much moisture, the ingredients will be stewed rather than being stir-fried.

Sometimes, the stir-fried dishes need thickening as a final step. To avoid getting a lumpy sauce, remove the wok or frying pan from the heat for a while before adding the thickening sauce.

## Deep-frying

Deep frying is another important Chinese cooking technique, producing foods with a crisp texture. Before deep-frying, the raw ingredients might need to be coated with corn starch. As it uses a lot of oil, deep frying is often thought of as an unhealthy cooking technique.  However, once the food is dropped into the hot oil, the outside surface will be "sealed", preventing any more oil being absorbed. Inside, the food will be cooked with the high heat.

Before starting, make sure the wok is stable or put it on a stand. Ensure the wok is no more than half filled with oil to avoid it spilling over.  Use a thermometer to check the temperature of the oil, or put a piece of bread into it.  The temperature will be at 180°C if the bread gets golden in 60 seconds. To prevent spitting, dry the ingredients before deep-frying. Use a pair of long wooden or bamboo chopsticks (not plastic chopsticks, as they will melt) to move the food as it is cooking, to stop it sticking together.

Finally, carefully remove the food with a large hand strainer and serve immediately, as it will quickly start to lose its crispness.

## Steaming

Steaming is a traditional Chinese cooking technique which, as it uses very little oil, is wonderful for preparing healthy meals. The food is cooked by the moist heat, retaining the nutrition, enhancing the natural flavour and bringing out the freshness of the ingredients. The perfect alternative for those that still consider that deep-fried food is unhealthy!

Steaming is suitable for all kinds of ingredients, such as meats, dumplings, dim sum and seafood, especially fish. The fresher the ingredients, the better they are for steaming.

When steaming, make sure the wok or container is stable, and the water does not touch the base of the steamer or rack. Place the heatproof plate with the ingredients to be steamed on the steamer or rack when the water is boiling, and place the lid on the wok. It is unnecessary to add water in the steam plate as the condensed steam and the seasonings sauces will give enough juice.

Remember to turn off the flame before attempting to take the lid off the wok, to avoid burning hands and arms in the hot steam.

## Shallow-frying

This technique uses more oil than stir-frying but less than deep-frying, while the temperature is lower than either of those two methods. Usually, the ingredients are cut into flat pieces and coated with batter. The food should be fried first on one side and then on the other. Finally, add some sauce to complete the dish. Shallow-fried food is tender inside and crisp outside. This technique is similar to sautéing, which is ideal for using a frying pan.

## Stewing

Stewing is a slow, moist cooking technique which is capable of turning the less tender cuts of meat to jelly-like tenderness.

Usually, the stewed ingredients are cut into small pieces and may consist of meats, fish and vegetables, as well as variety of seasonings. It generally requires just enough liquid to cover the food. Stewed food is different from soup in that it uses less liquid with a thicker consistency, takes longer and uses lower heat.

Throughout cooking process, the ingredients should be checked periodically to ensure the materials are not sticking to the base of the dish.

## Thickening

Thickening can be achieved by the addition of a thickening sauce. Typically, the thickening sauce is a blend of potato starch and water. Pour it in and stir fry with the ingredients to glaze the dish.

## Dressing

Dressing is also a cooking technique; it is the mixing the raw or unflavoured, cooked ingredients with variety of seasonings, such as sesame oil, red vinegar or soy sauce. Usually, the ingredients will be chopped into shreds, slices or pieces. It is similar to the process of preparing salad.

## Double-Boiling

Double boiling is a very popular cooking technique, especially for preparing canton soup. The required ingredients are placed into a ceramic container and covered with a lid. This is then placed into a wok which contains water, covered with the wok lid and boiled over a slow heat. It is perfect for retaining all the nutritional value of the ingredients in the container.

# Equipments

There are varieties of equipment being used in Chinese cooking. Most of them can be found in the normal home kitchen, but some of them are different from typical western cooking utensils.

### The Chinese Spatula
The Chinese Spatula is a long-handled spatula shaped like a shovel; it is used to toss and turn the ingredients when stir-frying in the wok. It is also useful for scooping the food to the dish.

### Ladle
This is a long-handled, bowl-shaped kitchen utensil which can be used to scoop soups and sauces.

### Wok Brush
A useful tool for cleaning the wok after used.

### The Chinese Wire Strainer
This utensil is ideal for removing noodles from boiling water or deep-fried foods from hot oil, as it allows the oil or liquid can be drained easily. The design of the long bamboo handle keeps the user away from the heat.

### Cleaver
In Chinese cooking, cutting food into uniform sizes is one of the most important skills. The Chinese cleaver can deal with all the cutting tasks such as slicing, shredding, chopping, crushing or mincing. Also, the end of the handle of the cleaver can be used to grind some ingredients. A high-carbon stainless steel cleaver is the best choice.

### Long Wooden Chopsticks
Besides using chopsticks during the meal, the Chinese also like to use long wooden chopsticks for putting ingredients into, and taking food out of, the wok. However, forks or ladles can be equally well used instead.

### Wok
The wok is the most basic Chinese cooking utensil in the Chinese kitchen. Almost all types of cooking techniques, such as stir-frying, deep-frying, shallow-frying, steaming or stewing, can be used in a wok. A round-bottomed wok is suitable for the gas stove, while the flat-bottomed type is perfectly for electric hob. The traditional uncoated carbon steel wok is still the best choice.

### Bamboo Steamer
This is used for steaming food and is designed to be placed inside the wok. It has been used for thousands of years in China. To use, first boil water in the wok then place the steamer, with the food, over the water. More than one layer of steamers can be used to steam more food at the same time.

### Chopping Block
You can find a wooden chopping block in any Chinese home kitchen. A wooden chopping block is much less slippery than a plastic one. After use, the chopping block should be scrubbed with hot water and it should be kept dry when it is not being used. Vinegar and lemon juice can be used as sanitizers to clean the chopping board occasionally.

### Steaming Stand or Rack
A stand or rack is a necessity when steaming foods in the wok. It ensures the food is kept above the water level, so that it is steamed, rather that boiled by direct contact with the water directly.

# Ingredients

# Noodles

### Fresh Noodles
Handmade noodle made from flour and water.

### Egg Noodles
Made from water, wheat flour and egg these
are the most common noodles in China.

### Dried flat noodles
Made from flour and water. The flat shape is easy
to clamp by chopstick.

### Dried buckwheat noodles
Made from buckwheat flour which contain
valuable nutrition.

### Cellaphane Noodles

Cellaphane noodles are made from mung bean flour, which appears in a clear colour. They become slippery after being cooked.

### Fresh Rice Noodles

Made with ground rice and water into a thick paste, steamed into a pastry-like flat piece, folded and cut into thick strips. Commonly used in restaurant for stir-frying.

### Chinese Vermicelli

Made from rice flour, Chinese vermicelli is often used with other ingredients, for Singapore fried noodle and soup noodles.

### Dried U-dong noodles

Also made from wheat flour and water but bigger size than other noodles. Popular in Japan.

# Vegetables

**Chinese Flowering Cabbage**
Chinese Flowering Cabbage, also called Choy Sum, has with tiny yellow flowers on the tips, light green leaves and pale green stems.

**Mustard Green**
Widely served stir-fried, blanched or in soups with other ingredients.

**Chinese White Cabbage**
Pak-choi is a leafy vegetable that has dark green leaves and white crisp ribs.

**Siu Pak Choi**
Sui Pak Choi is a vegetable similar to Chinese White Cabbage. It is better to choose one with white and firm stalks, and green crisp leaves.

**Chinese Broccoli**
Also called Gai Lan in Cantonese, Chinese Broccoli has long stems and green leaves. It is better to blanch the stalks before stir frying as they are a bit tough.

**Chinese Chives**
Looking like spring onions, Chinese Chives have slim, green stems. With a mild onion scent, chives are usually used for flavouring and garnishing seafood, meat or soups.

**Bean Sprouts**
Commonly used in stir fried dishes, the sprouts are germinated from green mung beans, growing from water controlled environment. They are more nutritious than the original beans

**Mange Tout**
It is a green flat pod common used for stir fried. Its sweet flavour goes excellent with meats and vegetables.

**Winter Melon**
This is a white gourd which is used in stir frying or often in soup with pork.

# Vegetables

**Water Spinach**
A hollow stem vegetable, water
spinach is delicious, especially stir-fried.

**Asparagus**
The thin, succulent stalks of asparagus
taste best when cooked on the day of
purchase. It is best to choose the ones
with firm, bright green stalks.

**Coriander**
Also called Chinese parsley which
is an annual herb with the green
leaves and often used to garnish
and season the food.

**Bamboo Shoots**
Conical, and light in colour, bamboo
shoots have a sweet taste when cooked.
Canned bamboo shoots can be cooked
without further preparation, but raw
bamboo shoots must be cut into slices
and cook in salted water until tender, or
else they will be noxious.

**Pickled Mustard Green**
A traditional Chinese pickled vegetable
which is often cooked with meat.

**Chinese Potherb Mustard**
A popular Chinese pickled vegetable
often used in stir-frying, cooking with
noodles and soups.

**Chinese Water Chestnut**
Also named "ma tai" in Cantonese,
Chinese water chestnut has a brown skin,
white flesh and crisp texture. It is highly
nutritious, and is particularly rich in protein
and vitamin C.

**Taro**
Light and dry taros are the best choice,
as the heavy ones will be too moist. After
being cooked, good taros will not be
floury, rather than tough.

**Golden Needles Mushrooms**
These are white mushrooms with
long and slender stems and firm,
white caps.

# Dried Products

### Wood Ear Fungi
Wood ear fungus is nutritious, though tasteless. However, the translucent brown flesh will fully absorb the flavours of other ingredients.

### Shiitake Mushroom
This edible fungus is normally found sun dried or fresh.

### Tangerine Peel
Dried status peel offering an orange flavour.

### Dried Shredded Seaweed
Dried shredded seaweed is rich in minerals, as it grows under the sea. It should be soaked in hot water until soft before use.

### Dried Longan
Longan is a small, round, yellow-skinned fruit. Inside, the pulp is white, sweet and soft.

### Dried Scallops
Dried scallops are a variety of dried seafood product that is very popular for making congee and soup.

### Hair Weed
Hair weed is threads of black dried vegetable. In Cantonese, they are called "Fat Choy". As this is homophonic for "Good Fortune". The surface of which becomes slippery after cooking. hair weed is a classic Chinese New Year festive ingredient.

### Laver
A kind of algae growing in the sea, Laver contains 29% to 35% of protein, iodine, a variety of vitamins and inorganic salts.

### Day Lily Buds
Day lily buds are yellow, with an earthy taste. They are often used in stir-fried dishes and soup.

**Mung Beans**
These small green beans are often used in Chinese cuisine, and can be used as other legumes.

**Soy Bean**
Mostly yellow appearance, soy beans are a valuable source of protein.

**Red Beans**
These oval beans are the main ingredient for making some delicious Chinese desserts.

**Puffed Bean Curd**
Puffed bean curd is pieces of deep-fried bean curd that readily absorbs the tastes and sauces of other ingredients.

**Fermented Bean Curd**
Made from soy beans, salt, rice wine and sesame oil.

**Fermented Black Beans**
Fermented black beans also called salted black beans which a fermented sauces having a distinctive flavour. It is widely used in Cantonese and Szechuan cuisines to season a steamed or stir fried dish.

**Tofu**
Also known as bean curd, tofu is made from soy milk. It looks like a soft cheese, is rich in protein but low in fat.

**Bean Curd Stick**
Also called dried tofu stick, this is the dried skin from the top of boiled soy milk.

**Bean Curd Sheet**
This is a thin and dried sheet of bean curd.

### Soy Sauce
Soy sauce is made from fermented soy beans and yeast, along with barley, salt and sugar.

### Oyster Sauce
Oyster sauce is made from oyster juice, sugar, salt, wheat flour and corn flour which is flavoured with oyster essence.

### Chilli Sauce
This is made from crushed chillies, salt and vinegar.

### Hoisin Sauce
Hoisin sauce is made from soy beans, wheat flour, potato starch, garlic, chilli peppers, sesame oil, salt, sugar and vinegar.

### Chilli Bean Sauce
This spicy, salty sauce is made from fermented soy beans and broad beans, salt and rice.

### Sesame Paste
Sesame paste is made from pulverised sesame seeds.

### Fish Sauce
This is made from fish, salt and water.

### Shrimp Paste
Shrimp paste is made from fermented and sun-dried ground shrimp.

### Black Bean Sauce
Made from fermented black beans, garlic and soy sauce, black bean sauce is a widely used seasoning.

### Fermented Yellow Soy Beans
Despite the appearance, the yellow fermented soy beans are the most commonly used ingredients for sauce making in many Chinese dishes.

### Sa Cha Sauce
Made from soy beans, shallots, chillies, garlic, brill and dried shrimp, this sauce has a slightly spicy taste.

### Szechuan Chilli Sauce
Made from chilli peppers, garlic, salt and spirit wine.

## Sauces, Wine and Vinegar

**Yellow Soy Bean Sauce**
A sauce made from yellow fermented soy beans, wheat flour, salt and water.

**Red Vinegar**
This is a popular vinegar in southern China; it is made from black, glutinous rice.

**Rice Vinegar**
This is a vinegar made from fermented rice and often used for cooking.

**Chilli Garlic Sauce**
A blend of ground chillies and garlic with a spicy taste.

**Rice Wine**
Rice wine is a spirit made from fermented rice and sugar.

**Sweet Bean Paste**
This is a sauce made from fermented soy beans, wheat flour, sugar and salt.

## Pastry Skins

**Dumpling skins**
Similar to, but thinner than, wonton skins, dumpling skins are round in shape. they are best steamed or boiled but not deep-fried.

**Wonton Skins**
These are thin sheets made from the eggs and flour, especially for making wonton and siu mai.

**Spring Roll Skins**
Made from wheat flour and water, especially for making spring roll.

42

# Herbs & Spices

**Szechuan Peppercorns**
It is spicy to numb which is a very popular ingredient in the Szechuan cuisine.

**Dried Birdseye Chilli**
Have a strong scent and very spicy when cooked with a dish, which is mainly used in Szechuan cuisine.

**Five-spice Powder**
A mixture of spices powder which including ground star anise, cinnamon, fennel seeds, cloves and Szechuan peppercorns.

**White Sesame Seeds**
It is the white seeds from the sesame plant which is often used in garnishing the food.

**Star Anise**
It is an eight-pointed star spice with liquorice flavour.

**Sha Ginger**
An essential seasoning material used to counteract any rank odour of other ingredients.

**Wolfberry**
It is a variety of wild bush which contains a high value of nutrients. Chinese people enjoy using wolfberry to make tea, soup and wine etc.

**Cumin**
A kind of aromatic seeds which can be found as powder form or as a whole.

**Lemongrass**
Commonly used as marinade herb in meat and seafood, its distinctive flavour adds a different dimension in curry and grilled meats.

# Herbs and Spices

**Mix Spices**
The packets used to make the marinade sauce including star anise, Szechuan peppercorns, ginger, fennel, cardamom, cinnamon, cloves and liquorice.

**Ginseng**
It is a smooth perennial herb, which consists of fleshy and slow-growing roots.

**Bay Leaves**
A variety of culinary herbs which is green and oval-shaped with a sweet scent. It can help to enhance the flavour of the dishes.

**Almonds**
The fruit seed of the almond tree, which contains valuable nutrition and has many benefits for people.

**Chinese Yam**
A herb which has a sweet flavour and is Yin & Yang balance.

**Ginkgo Nuts**
Tender nuts from Gingko tree, which will have a sweet taste after being cooked.

# Good Hygiene Practices

## 1) Safe Handling food

In order to prevent causing food poisoning, careful time and temperature control is essential.

When preparing food, keep it out of the fridge for the shortest time as food poisoning bacteria multiply at temperatures between 5C to 63C. Cook food thoroughly until it is piping hot as high temperatures can be used to destroy pathogenic micro-organisms in food. If you have leftover food, cool food as quickly as possible and store them in the fridge. When you reheat the food make sure that the food is steaming hot thoroughly and reheat only once because more times you cool and reheat a food, the higher risk of food poisoning.

The use of different colour code chopping boards for raw food and for ready-to-eat food is recommended. As raw foods can contain harmful bacteria that can spread very easily to anything they touch, including other foods, worktops, chopping boards and knives.

Wash worktops before and after preparing food, particularly after they have been touched by raw meat, raw eggs, fish and vegetables. Clean tea towels regularly. Dirty damp cloths can contaminate your food by spreading bacteria. Disposable paper wiping cloths are preferred.

## 2) Safe Food Storage

Obtaining food from a reliable source is the first step to prevent food from risk of contamination. Make sure foods are fresh and within the date code. Raw and high risk foods are must be stored separately in the fridge immediately after purchase. Failure to ensure correct storage conditions will result in food contamination and multiplication of bacteria.

Highly perishable food with a use by date, such as dairy products and cooked meat goes off quite quickly. Any food that has passed this date is likely to be dangerous to eat. And it is against the law to sell or serve food that has gone beyond a use by date.

Less perishable food with a best before date, such as frozen food, dried food and canned food with a longer life. It should be safe to eat but may not be at its best quality after this date.

## Chilled Food

The effective chilled storage temperatures of the refrigerators usually operate between 1C to 4C because most bacteria cannot multiply or multiply very slowly at this refrigerator temperature. If large quantity of foods is loaded into the fridge, temperature will rises. Never put hot food in a refrigerator. It will also raises the temperature of the refrigerator and may create condensation, which can cause contamination by dripping onto other food.

As a good practice, High risk food, milk dessert and cream cakes should be kept on the top shelf of the refrigerator, ready-to-eat food on second and third shelf. Raw meat and poultry should be stored on a low shelf to avoid any risk of contamination from dripping juice or blood onto other foods. All foods should be covered to avoid drying-out, absorption of odour and cross-contamination.

Once you open can foods, transfer the contents into a storage container as the metal of the can may transfer to the can's contents. Never keep open can in the fridge.

Clean and disinfect fridge regularly.

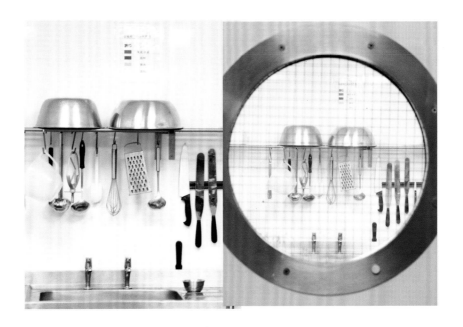

# Good Hygiene Practices

### Frozen food

Freezers should operate at -18C or slightly below. At this temperature, food will keep for a reasonable time with no bacteria growth. However, bacteria will survive and if the temperature rises above -10C, especially moulds and yeast, begin to develop. Therefore, any food purchased should be stored in the freezer as quickly as possible and must not kept for longer than recommended by manufacturer, as the quality gradually deteriorates.

When you freeze meat and fish, freeze it before their use by date and defrost thoroughly before cooking. And make sure they are properly wrapped to prevent freezer burn and contamination.

Frozen meat and fish should be thawed on the bottom shelf of the refrigerator. However, if you want to cook straight away, you can use microwave to defrost. Never re-freeze thawed food.

### 3) Personal Hygiene

Most people carry some type of organism, especially when they have diarrhoea and/or vomiting. Because our body temperature is 37C, it is ideal for the growth of bacteria. These organisms can easily be transferred from your hand and cause illness. Therefore, hands must be kept clean at all times. Especially:

After visiting toilet

After handling raw meat, including eggs, and before handling ready-to-eat food

After touching your hair or face.

After coughing or sneezing into your hands or handkerchief.

After dealing with waste food or refuse.

After touching animal and cleaning up their faeces.

After cleaning, or handling dirty cloths, crockery, etc.

# Handwashing Procedure

As the hands are directly contact with food, they are most common way of transferring food poisoning bacteria. In order to prevent contamination of food, the correct hand washing procedure is necessary. You must wash your hands thoroughly and properly.

1) Wash your hand in (35°C-40°C) warm running water.

2) Use disinfectant soap.

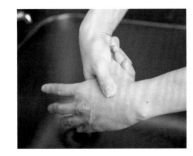

3) Applied sufficient liquid soap to ensure a good lather.

4) Rub between fingers.

5) Rub thumbs.

6) Finger tips.

7) Rub palms

8) The wrists

9) Rinse thoroughly in warm water to remove all the lather, bacteria and dirt.

It is essential to use disposable paper towel to dry your hand after washing to reduce the number of bacteria remaining. And water taps must be cleaned as well.

## Food poisoning

Food poisoning is mainly caused by eating food contaminated by pathogenic bacteria. In order to cause food poisoning, large numbers of pathogenic micro-organisms are needed. The bacteria multiply to levels that cause illness when the food is kept in a warm room which is the ideal conditions for bacterial multiplication. In this condition, each bacterium needs just 10 to 20 minutes to multiply, so 1,000 bacteria can become 1,000,000+ in 1hour 40mins.

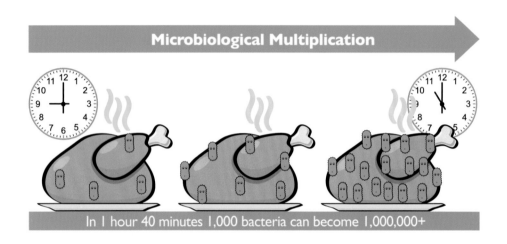

Persons who eat contaminated food can suffer from food poisoning and they have symptoms such as abdominal pain, diarrhoea and vomiting which can last one to seven days. It is usually occurs within one to 36 hours of eating contaminated food. The most at risk include the elderly, persons who are already ill or recovering, and pregnant women and their unborn babies.

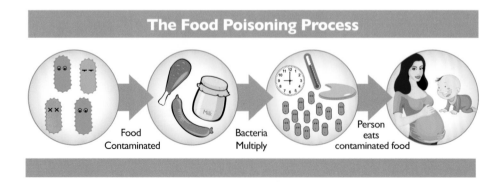

# The Germometer

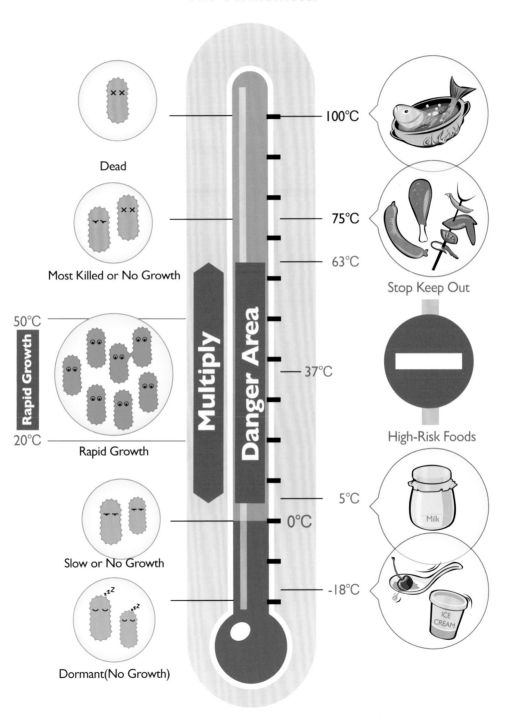

Dead

Most Killed or No Growth

Rapid Growth

50°C

20°C

Rapid Growth

Slow or No Growth

Dormant(No Growth)

Multiply

Danger Area

100°C

75°C

63°C

37°C

5°C

0°C

-18°C

Stop Keep Out

High-Risk Foods

前菜

菜譜

# Appetizer

# Aromatic Crispy Duck

Aromatic crispy duck is a famous Szechuan dish. Along with crisp skin and tender meat, the aroma of this dish is particular distinctive.

## Serves 8-10

### Ingredients
1 fresh duck 2.5kg (5½lb)
2 litres vegetable oil (for frying)
600ml (1 pint) water for poaching

### Seasoning
5 slices of ginger cut in 2mm thick
100g shallots
5g Szechuan peppercorns
2 star anise
5g Allspice (ground)
3 tablespoons light soy sauce
1 tablespoon sugar
½ teaspoon salt (optional)
½ tablespoon rice wine
1 tablespoon sesame seed oil

### Sauce
1 tablespoon soy bean paste
2 tablespoons Hoi-sin sauce
2 teaspoons sesame seed oil
1 teaspoon sugar
Mixed all together into thin sauce

### Condiments
1-2 packets of duck pancake
1 cucumber peeled and cut to
   5-6cm long pieces, cut vertically
   again to the size of a chopstick
Spring onion or leek (white part)
   cut into similar length as the
   cucumber, then finely cut again
   vertically.

## Method

- Clean and dry the duck thoroughly. Cut the duck in half between the breasts, then run the knife through the skin above the leg, separating the breast from the leg without cutting through the breast meat to give 4 quarters.

- Put all the seasonings (which seasonings) and water in a large cooking pot, put all 4 duck quarters into the pot, bring to the boil then lower to medium heat, cover with the lid and let it poach for 2 ½ hours. Make sure the liquid in the pot does not spill over.

- After poaching, carefully remove each quarter and place onto a large dish to drain off any excess liquid. When cooled, use kitchen paper towel to make sure no liquid left (this is to avoid oil spitting when deep-frying). The duck is now ready to for the final stage of cooking.

- In an electric deep-fryer, pour in around 2 litres of vegetable oil (but always check the manufacturer's information for the correct volume of oil to be used). Heat the oil on the highest setting and place the duck carefully into the fryer. Depending on the capacity of the fryer, its best to fry only one or 2 pieces at a time - do not attempt to put all 4 quarters into the fryer, as this will lower the oil temperature and prolong the cooking process. Fry until the duck skin becomes dry and crisp: it should be firm and brittle when tapped with a fork.

- Finally, drain off the excess oil, use 2 forks to tear the meat into small pieces, warm up the duck pancakes with a food steamer or microwave oven and serve with the listed condiments and sauce.

*Useful tip:* If preparing ahead of a dinner party, you can wrap the poached duck with cling-film and store them in a fridge for up to 48 hours, make sure to add 2 more minutes when deep-frying.

# Bang Bang Chicken

A traditional Szechuan dish, the name reflects the fact that the chicken meat is softened by 'banging' with a meat hammer. The technique allows different fragranced oils and sauces to permeate the chicken, combining hot, sour, sweet, salty, heat and cold. This dish is served cold.

## Serves 5

### Ingredient
500g boneless chicken meat

### Seasoning
1 1/2 tablespoon sesame seed oil
2 tablespoons chilli oil
1 teaspoon Szechuan peppercorn
2 tablespoons sesame seed paste or tahini
1 tablespoon light soy sauce
1 teaspoon of sugar
2 tablespoons red rice vinegar
10g finely chopped spring onion
2 slices of ginger, for chicken stock

### Sauce
Use 5 tablespoons of cold chicken stock to dilute the sesame seed paste, mixed in all the oils, sugar and vinegar. Add the finely chopped spring onion and ginger

### Condiments
1 teaspoon toasted sesame seeds
1 cucumber peeled and cut to 5-6cm long strips, cut finely vertically again to the size of a chopstick,
1 medium hot red chilli, deseeded
Use the white part of spring onion, cut into 5-6cm long strips, finely cut them vertically again, immerse in a small bowl of cold water to let them turn curly, drain and leave them for garnish
2-3 sprigs of coriander

## Method
- Boil 2 cups of water in a cook pot and add 2 slices of ginger.

- Place the chicken in the boiling water, poach the chicken on a high heat for 10 minutes, then turn the chicken over and poach another 10 minutes.

- Meanwhile, fill a large bowl with ice and 2 cups of drinking water. Then, using a bamboo strainer or perforated ladle, take the chicken from the boiling water and place in the ice water for 10 minutes.

- Dry the chicken in kitchen paper towel and, spreading it as evenly as possible, place it into a large food bag or cling film. Use a meat hammer or rolling pin to 'Bang' the cooked meat until tender.

- In a large serving dish, tear the chicken meat in bite-size pieces, saturate the meat with the sauce prepared earlier, add the cucumber and red chilli and mix thoroughly.

- Before serving, sprinkle with a few drops of sesame seed oil and toasted sesame seeds, then garnish with the curly spring onion and chopped coriander.

# Deep-fried Whitebaits

Deep-fried Whitebaits is a dish that is an ideal appetizer, this dish is very easy to prepare and cook. Crispy but light in taste, it is the perfect appetizer for alcoholic drinks, congee or for eating as a snack.

## Serves 5

### Ingredient

500g (1lb) whitebaits cleaned and dried,
100g self-raising flour for batter
2 litres Vegetable cooking oil for frying

### Seasoning

3 slices ginger, finely chopped
½ teaspoon salt
¼ teaspoon white-ground pepper
1 spring onion, finely chopped

### Condiments

Curly spring onion, use the green part, finely cut in strips vertically. Put in a small bowl of cold water to make the ends curl up, use them for garnish.
A pinch of Sea-salt

## Method

- Place all the whitebaits in a colander, wash then stand on a dish or bowl to drain off excess liquid. Use all the seasonings to marinate the fish for about 30 minutes.

- Meanwhile, prepare the batter for frying. Add enough cold water to the self-raising flour to ensure the batter is not too thick - a consistency like pancake batter is perfect for frying.

- Heat the cooking oil in an electric deep-fryer to 180°C, put all the marinated whitebaits into the batter, make sure the fish are coated from head to tail, place a small handful into the heated oil, separating them as you drop into the oil so that they don't stick together. Fry until the batter to light yellow in colour, remove from the fryer and drain off excess oil on paper towel. Fry the rest of the fish in the same way.

- Reheat the oil if necessary then, again in batches, fry the fish a second time until golden brown or until the batter is crispy in texture.

- Decorate the course with curly spring onion and sea salt as to your personal preference.

*Useful tips: The second-frying shouldn't last too long, in case the fishes became dry and burn.*

# Prawn on Toast

A popular Hong Kong afternoon tea sandwich, local chefs invented this dish to replace normal sandwiches to serve at high tea. Using mainly fresh prawn to make, this dish grew far more popular with the general public than its colonial history intended.

## Serves 2

### Ingredient

100g fresh or frozen uncooked prawns, keep 2 aside for decoration, peel the prawns, use a small sharp knife to score the back of the prawn to remove the vein. Wash and dry the prawns on kitchen paper towel.

Remove shell from the remaining 2 prawns, but keep the tails, cut in half, keep the tail part for decoration, use the top part with the rest of the prawns

½ medium grated onion

2 slices ginger, grated

2 slices of fresh bread, cut away all edges

1 medium egg

1 tablespoon sesame seeds

### Seasoning

⅛ teaspoon salt

¼ teaspoon sugar

½ teaspoon cornflour

½ teaspoon sesame seed oil

### Condiments

2 lettuce leaves

## Method

■ Remove the shells and de-vein the raw prawns. If frozen prawns are used, defrost thoroughly.

■ Mince the raw prawns with the back of a cleaver or meat knife. Add the grated onion, ginger, cornstarch and chicken stock and mix into a paste texture.

■ Spread the paste generously on top of both slices of bread.

■ Beat the egg in a small bowl, then brush the prawn paste side thinly with egg and evenly coat with sesame seeds to cover the top.

■ Use a 4cm round pastry cutter to cut each slice of bread into 3 rounds to give 6 small pieces in total.

■ Decorate 2 rounds with the half prawn with the tail side up, press the prwan in the centre as illustrated.

■ In an electric deep-fryer, heat the oil to 150°C using the recommended minimum volume, place the triangles in the fryer and turn the heat down to medium to let them fry slowly for 4 minutes or until golden brown in colour. Turn the toast regularly during frying to prevent burning on one side.

■ Drain excess oil on a kitchen paper towel. Serve on the lettuce leaves.

*Useful tips:* You can also minced the prawns in a food processor. if preferred, you can cut the bread in any shape.

# Deep Fried Cabbage

A highly nutritious appetizer and very easy to make.

## Serves 10

### Ingredient
500g Spring Green

### Seasoning
½ teaspoon sea salt

### Condiments
1 tablespoon toast-dried fish (optional)

## Method

- Clean the spring Green leaves and remove the leaf stalks.

- Drain off excess water in a colander. Finely shredded all the leaves, ensure the leaves are completely dry before cooking.

- In an electric deep-fryer, using the recommended maximum volume, heat the oil to 190°C, place all the shredded leave a small handful inside the fryer to fry for 7 minutes or until crisp. Remove them with a wired strainer and drain off excess oil on kitchen paper towel. Fry the rest of the shredded leaves in the same way.

- Before serving, sprinkle a little sea salt and garnish with one tablespoon toast-dried fish.

# Deep Fried Won Ton

This humble snack can be traced back in Chinese history for more than 2000 year. Every region has its own version of Won Ton(or wonton): steamed, fried, baked, for example. The cantonese soup version is the most popular of all. This recipe, has been enhanced with extra vegetable that taste best by fried.

## Serves 8-10

### Ingredient

1 packet of wonton skin (40 sheets)
350g fresh minced pork
100g uncooked minced prawn
100g tin sweetcorn kernels, drain and
    keep dry
100g carrot grated
2 large spring onion finely chopped
1 medium egg

### Seasoning

½ teaspoon ground pepper
1 teaspoon salt
2 teaspoons light soy sauce
½ teaspoon sesame seed oil
½ teaspoon sugar

### Condiments

Sweet chilli sauce

## Method

- Put the minced pork, prawn, sweet corn kernels, grated carrot and finely chopped onion in a large bowl. Pour in all the seasonings and beaten egg and use a serving spoon to mix the ingredients well.

- Place one sheet of wonton skin on a large plate and scoop one teaspoonful of the mixed raw meat in the centre of the wonton skin. Bring the 4 corners of the sheet together, squeeze and twist to close to make a little parcel. Do not over-fill the sheet, as the technique is intended to seal the moisture of the filling inside the wonton skin. Finish wrapping the rest of the wonton skins in the same way, then cover the plate with cling film or a tea towel.

- In an electric deep-fryer, heat the oil to 150°C using the recommended maximum volume. When the oil is heated, place 6 to 8 pieces of wonton parcel in the fryer (8 to 10 if using a large fryer). Fry until the wonton have turned golden brown.

- Drain off the excess oil on kitchen paper towel. Serve with sweet chilli sauce as a dip.

# Vegetarian Spring Rolls

Spring rolls derived from a traditional spring festival cake as far back as Han Dynasty. During the Ming Dynasty, spring rolls were served as the 9th course of imperial banquets lasting 128 courses. From region to region, spring rolls are made in different sizes and shapes and various meat or vegetables fillings.

## Serves 8

## Ingredients
1 packet frozen pancake skin (16 sheets)

## Filling
300g tin bamboo shoot, drained and cut into
    5cm strips and thinly cut again vertically
4 Chinese mushrooms, soaked and dried,
    remove stems, cut into thin slices. Half tin
    if ready cut tin mushroom are used.
100g Chinese chives, clean and cut into 5 cm
    length
1 carrot peeled and grated
2 cloves of finely chopped garlic
1 teaspoon cornflour for thickening
20g plain flour for making paste to seal the
    spring roll skin

## Seasoning
½ teaspoon ground pepper
1 teaspoon salt
2 teaspoons light soy sauce
½ teaspoon sesame seed oil
½ teaspoon sugar
½ tablespoon Worcester sauce

*Useful tips: Add minced pork, chicken or duck to make up your choice of the filling, just reduce the vegetable to half.*

*The filling will expand a little during cooking, make sure you don't overfill the roll.*

## Method
- Briefly blanch the cut bamboo shoots and carrot in a pot of boiling water, drain and put to one side.

- Heat the wok until smoke appears when cooking oil is added, fry the chopped garlic and mushroom for 2 minutes, add the bamboo shoots, carrot and Chinese chives and fry for a further 3 minutes. Add salt, sugar, light soy sauce and sesame seed oil to the wok and mix well. Dilute the cornstarch with Worcester sauce and 2 tablespoons of water, pour in the vegetable mixture and cook until the liquid is completely absorbed.

- Put the vegetables into a colander and spread out to let any excess liquid drain out. Leave them to completely cool off.

- Mix the plain flour with little water to form a paste.

- Defrost the pancake skin, carefully separating the pancake skins one at a time. Lay the pancake skin diagonally and put 2 tablespoons of the vegetable filling horizontally near the bottom of the skin. Next, fold the bottom to cover the filling, fold both sides of the skin over to make sure all the fillings are tucked inside, brush a little flour paste on the far side of the pancake skin and roll the pancake into the shape of a tube. Finish making all the rolls in the same way.

- In an electric deep-fryer, heat the oil to 150°C using the recommended maximum volume, when the oil is heated, place a few rolls at a time into the fryer and fry until golden brown. Drain excess oil and serve hot.

# Peking Spare Ribs

A traditional meat dish, beloved by the people from the old imperial city Peking (now called Beijing), hence the name.

## Serves 4

## Main Ingredient
500g fresh pork spare ribs

## Marinade
1 tablespoon light soy sauce
1 tablespoon rice cooking wine
10g finely chopped ginger
50g plain flour (for coating)
1 medium egg (for coating)

## Seasoning
2 cloves of garlic finely chopped
2 tablespoons light soy sauce
1 tablespoon rice cooking wine
4 tablespoons sugar
2 tablespoon Dark rice vinegar
1 teaspoon chilli sauce
1 tablespoon sesame seed oil
100ml water
1 tablespoon cornflour
Mixed all the above thoroughly and keep
   aside

## Condiments
Chopped spring onion
1 sprig of coriander

## Method

- Using a meat cleaver to chop the spare ribs into 5-8cm pieces. In a large bowl, marinade the spare ribs well with soy sauce, rice wine and chopped ginger. Cover the bowl with cling film and keep in the refrigerator for at least 15 minutes.

- Before the first stage of cooking, beat an egg and pour into the spare ribs, blended well first then coat the spare ribs with plain flour.

- In an electric deep-fryer, heat the oil to 180°C using the recommended minimum volume. When the oil is heated, place the spare ribs in the fryer to cook for 10 minutes.

- Remove the spare ribs from the fryer and drain off excess oil on kitchen paper towel.

- Heat a wok or frying pan over a high heat, add 1 tablespoon vegetable cooking oil and the chopped garlic, put the spare ribs in the wok and stir-fried for 3 minutes. Mix the prepared seasoning well and add in the work and keep stirring for 2 minutes. Before serving the spare ribs on a plate, add chopped spring onion and diluted cornflour to mix for 30 second or until the sauce thickens. Serve at once.

*Useful tips:* *Depends on the capacity of your fryer, you can fry the spare ribs in batch. If you prefer the spare ribs with sauce, reduce the amount of cornflour to half.*

# Satay Chicken on Skewers

A favourite South East Asian street food, the secret of this dish is the sauce and the aroma of char-grilled chicken: the two are a match made in heaven. The story of an Indonesian man who was so fond of eating satay chicken, he pawned his sarong to get money to buy this food is still being told in Indonesia.

## Serves 4

### Main Ingredient

450g fresh boneless chicken legs
½ green pepper
½ red pepper
1 pack of bamboo skewers

### Seasoning

2 tablespoons Satay sauce
2 tablespoons light soy sauce
1 tablespoon rice wine
1 teaspoon sesame seeds oil
½ teaspoon chilli powder

### Sauce

2 tablespoons Satay sauce
1 tablespoon crunchy peanut butter
1 teaspoon light soy sauce
1 teaspoon sugar
4 tablespoons water
½ teaspoon cornflour

## Method

- Discard the skin from chicken and cut them in 3-4cm cubes.

- Marinade the chicken in a bowl with all the seasonings, mixed well, then cover the bowl with cling film and keep the chicken in the refrigerator for a day.

- Before cooking the chicken, cut both green and red peppers into pieces of similar size to the chicken.

- Skewer 3 chicken cubes between a piece of green and a piece of red pepper.

- Preheat the grill to 240°C, lay a large piece of foil on the bottom of the grill pan and brush a little oil on the grill-rack before laying the meat vertically on top.

- Turn the heat down to 180°C, grill the chicken for 7 minutes on one side, turn and grill the other side for 5 minutes. Place the cooked chicken on a serving dish.

- Blend all the sauce ingredients thoroughly in a saucepan, heat the mixture until thickens, pour over the chicken skewers and serve.

*Useful tips:* Add dried chilli flakes or chilli powder on the chicken before grilling if you like the satay hot.

# Yuk Sung

This dish is a perfect food for party, instead of pastry and bread canapés, try this tasty bite size appetizer; its light, refreshing and very easy to make.

## Serves 4

### Main Ingredient

200g fillet of pork, coarsely cut to small pieces

4 fresh Chinese mushrooms, rehydrated by boiling in water first if using dried mushrooms.

80g tin water chestnut (drained weight) cut to small pieces

80g tin bamboo shoot (drained weight) cut to small pieces

½ finely chopped onion

### Marinade

½ teaspoon salt

1 teaspoon corn flour

1 teaspoon rice wine

### Seasoning

1 clove of garlic crushed and finely chopped

2 teaspoons light soy sauce

1 teaspoon sesame seeds oil

2 tablespoons oyster sauce

½ teaspoon salt

Little ground pepper

1 sprig spring onion, finely chopped

### Condiments

2 tablespoons Hoi sin sauce

Iceberg lettuce

## Method

■ Wash and dry the lettuce, discard a few outer leaves, then cut the lettuce ball in half and half again, loosen the leaves and only use the bowl shape leaves.

■ Marinade the pork for half an hour with salt, rice wine and corn flour before cooking.

■ Remove the stems from the mushrooms, squeeze out execss water if using rehydrated mushrooms. Cut into small pieces.

■ Preheat a wok until smoke rises, pour in 1 tablespoon of vegetable cooking oil, then add garlic and onion to stir for 30 second, add the meat to blend in for 2 minutes, then add the Chinese mushrooms, water chestnuts and bamboo shoots and blends all the ingredients in the wok vigorously. Finally, add salt, oyster sauce, light soy sauce, ground pepper. When the liquid has evaporated, add chopped spring onion and sesame oil to stir for 20 seconds.

■ Serves the meat in the middle of a serving dish, with the lettuce arranged around. If preferred, spoon the cooked meat into individual pieces of lettuce as illustrated and served them on a canapé dish.

# Soups

# Chicken and Sweet Corn Soup

This delicious soup is served at almost all Chinese restaurants worldwide. You can either use tinned or fresh sweet corn to make this soup, though using creamed sweet corn from tin is probably the easiest way.

## Serves 4-5

### Ingredients
100g boneless chicken breast
1 tin of cream sweet corn or
4 freshsweet corn cobs
1 litre of water
1 medium egg

### Seasoning
½ teaspoon salt
A pinch of ground pepper
¼ teaspoon sesame seed oil

### Thickening
1 teaspoon corn flour
2 tablespoons of water

## Method

■ Steam or Boil the chicken breast meat for 15 minute in 1 cup of water. When the chicken is cooked, removed it from the water and let it cool. Keep the liquid for making soup later.

■ Diced the chicken to small pieces and put to one side.

■ If using fresh sweet corn cobs, first use a small, sharp knife to slice off the corn kernels. Next liquidise the corn kernels in a blender using the water used to cook the chicken. (If using tinned sweet corn as a substitute, liquidise the corn in the blender slightly).

■ In a large saucepan, boil 1.5 litre of water then, saving a lile diced chicken as a garnish, add the rest of the diced chicken and creamed sweet corn and simmer for 15 minutes, stirring continuously to prevent starch built up at the bottom of the saucepan. If using creamed sweet corn, reduce the simmer time to 3 minutes. Add all the seasoning ingredients.

■ Before adding the corn flour to thicken soup, beat the egg in a small bowl and put on one side.

■ Turn the heat up slightly to the boiling point, mix the corn flour with 2 tablespoons of water, then pour the liquid in the saucepan while stirring the soup constantly to produce a chowder-like consistency. Drizzle the beaten egg into the soup while stirring the soup gently. 。

■ Serve the soup in soup bowls, garnished with the diced chicken on top. Serve immediately.

# Hot and Sour Soup

A classic Szechuan dish, Hot and sour Soup is a popular soup served at almost every Chinese restaurant. The piquant flavour of the dark Chinese vinegar and fiery spicy taste of the white pepper and red, green chillies awakens your taste buds before you start to eat your main course.

## Serves 4-5

### Ingredient

20g reconstituted and shredded
   woodear fungi
20g shredded bamboo shoots
20g shredded pickled mustard plant
5g shredded medium hot red chilli
5g shredded medium hot green chilli
15g small frozen Shrimps (defrosted)
15g frozen peas (defrosted)
1 litre of water
1 medium egg
1 spring onion finely chopped

### Seasoning

½ teaspoon salt
1 tablespoon chilli paste
1½ tablespoon Chinese dark vinegar
½ teaspoon sesame seed oil
½ teaspoon white ground pepper

### Thickening

1 teaspoon corn flour2 tablespoons
   water

## Method

- Beat the egg in a small bowl and keep aside. Finely chop the spring onion and keep for garnish.

- Boil 1 litre of water in a saucepan. Add the main ingredients and simmer for 5 minutes, then add the seasoning ingredients and simmer for further one minute.

- Turn the heat up and bring the soup to the boil. Mix the corn flour with 2 tablespoons water and stir the liquid into the soup; the soup should be in a loose consistency.

- Drizzle the beaten egg into the soup and keep stirring.

- Serve the soup in soup bowl, garnished with chopped spring onion.

# Dom Yam Soup

Another spicy and sour soup, dom yam soup is widely served in Southeast Asian countries. The name "Tom" means soup in Tai language spoken by Thai and Lao. "Yam" means spicy and sour.

## Serves 2

### Ingredient

6 fresh prawns with shell
4 mussels
75g fresh squid
1 medium tomato, peeled & deseeded
400ml of water
¼ teaspoon tamarind paste (optional)
½ red chilli
1 spring onion

### Seasoning

⅓ teaspoon salt
½ teaspoon fish sauce (optional)
¼ teaspoon white-ground pepper
⅓ teaspoon sesame seed oil

### Condiments

Coriander

## Method

- Wash and dry the prawns, mussels and squid. Cut the squid in 4cm squares and score the surface slightly vertically then again horizontally.

- Peel the tomato and deseed then dice into small pieces.

- Remove seeds from chilli and cut the chilli in rings. Cut the spring onion into 2cm lengths.

- Boil the water in saucepan and add all the ingredients and simmer for 3 minutes. Add salt, ground white pepper and sesame seed oil to taste. Serve at once.

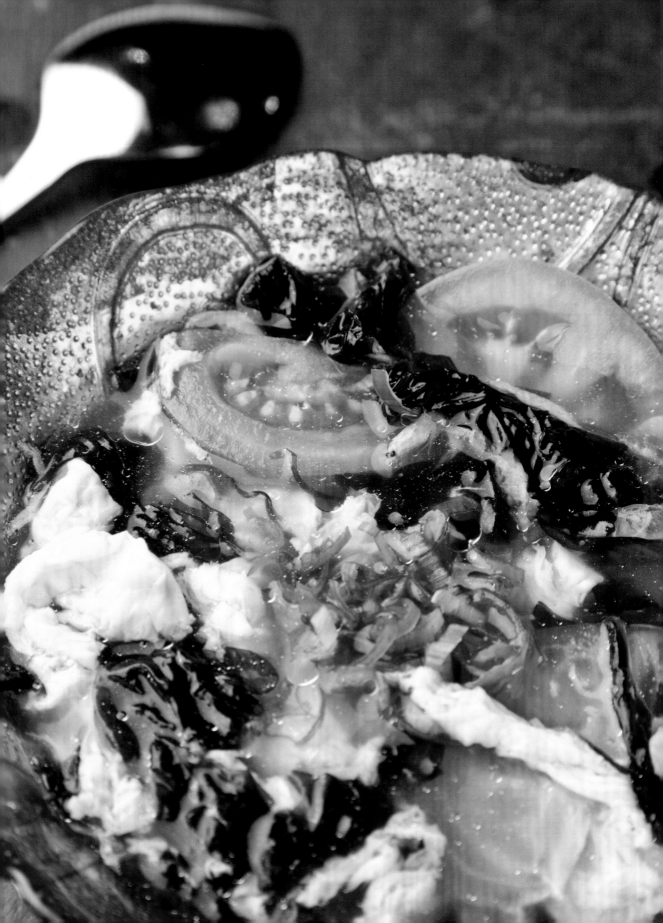

# Seaweed Soup

Seaweed soup is a classic Cantonese soup, highly nutritious and quick to prepare. The egg drops gives the soup a very smooth taste.

## Serves 2-3

### Ingredient

75g dried seaweed
1 tomato
1 medium egg
1 spring onion finely chopped
500ml water

### Seasoning

⅓ teaspoon salt
¼ teaspoon sesame seed oil
¼ teaspoon white ground pepper

## Method

- Cut the tomato in half, cut again in slices. Finely chop the spring onion and put to one side for garnish. Beat the egg in a small bowl.

- Boil 500ml water in a saucepan. Add the seaweed and tomato and simmer for 2 minutes. Add all the seasoning ingredients.

- Turn the heat up to boil the soup, drizzle the beaten egg into the soup and keep stirring.

- Garnish the soup with chopped spring onion and serve immediately.

# West Lake Beef Soup

A stunning looking soup with intense flavours of beef and coriander. This soup is named after the famous West Lake in Hangzhou, where generations of poets and artists came to admire the picturesque scenery.

## Serves 4-5

### Ingredient

100g lean beef preferably fillet steak
75g tofu
25g button mushrooms
15g coriander stalks
1 medium egg
750ml water

### Seasoning

½ teaspoon salt
½ teaspoon sesame seed oil
¼ teaspoon white ground pepper
½ teaspoon corn flour
1 teaspoon of vegetable cooking oil

### Thickening

1 teaspoon corn flour
3 tablespoons water

## Method

- Wash the coriander then keep a couple leaves aside for garnishing, remove the leaves from the rest of the coriander and finely chopped them.

- Cut the beef into small slices then use a meat cleaver to chop the beef into minced beef. Marinade the minced beef with half teaspoon of corn flour and one teaspoon of oil.

- Dice the tofu and mushrooms to small pieces.

- Beat the egg in a small bowl.

- Boil 750ml water in a saucepan then keeping the heat in moderately high, add tofu, mushroom, chopped coriander and minced beef to the saucepan. Stir well and add all the seasoning ingredients.

- Mix 1 teaspoon corn flour with 3 tablespoons of water. Pour the liquid into the saucepan and stir well, then drizzle the egg into the soup while still stirring. The soup is now ready to serve.

# ABC Soup

ABC soup is easy to cook, yet healthy and delicious. It is called because it is as easy as ABC.

## Serves 2-3

### Ingredient
400g pork spare ribs
1 tomato
1 potato
1 carrot
1 leek
2 celery stalks
75g button mushroom
1 spring onion finely chopped
1.5 litre of water

### Seasoning
½ teaspoon salt
½ teaspoon sesame seed oil
¼ teaspoon white ground pepper

## Method

- Wash and chop the spare rib into 4cm pieces.

- Wash and peel the carrot and potato, then cut both into chunks. Cut the tomato into quarters.

- Cut the celery stalks and leek into 4cm lengths and cut the button mushrooms into halves. Finely chop the spring onion and keep aside.

- Boil 1.5 litre of water, add the spare rib and simmer for one and half hour. Add all the ingredients and seasonings and simmer for 30 minutes. Garnish with chopped spring onion and serve immediately.

# Chicken Herbal Soup

Herbal soup is a traditional Chinese 'Food Remedy' to promote good health. It is often recommended by Chinese herbalists for consumption in the autumn and winter months. With the warmth of the Chinese yam and wolfberries, and the protein from chicken, it is an ideal energy food. This soup can also be steamed in a hot pot.

## Serves 2-3

### Ingredients

½ organic chicken
50g Chinese dried yam
20g wolfberries
1 clove of garlic
2 slices of ginger
1.5 litre of water

### Seasoning

½ teaspoon salt

## Method

- Cut the chicken in 4 large pieces. Wash the Chinese yam and wolfberries.

- Boil 1.5 litre of water in a saucepan, add all the ingredients and seasoning, bring to boil and simmer for 90 minutes in low heat.

- Because this soup will take more than an hour to cook, the grease content will release from the chicken skin. If you prefer less grease in the soup, you can either remove the skin before cooking or skim off the grease from the surface of the soup before serving.

# Steamed Ginseng Soup

Steaming soup is a traditional, though lengthy, way of preparing herbal soup. The technique allows both meat and herbs to slowly release their flavours without vaporising through cooking.

## Serves 2-3

## Ingredients
½ organic chicken (remove skin if preferred)
1 whole ginseng
2 Chinese mushrooms
10g wolfberries
2 slices of ginger
1 spring onion
1 litre of water

## Seasoning
½ teaspoon salt

## Method
- Wash all the ingredients and drain off excess water. Discard the green part of the spring onion then cut the white part into 2 pieces.

- Use a very large saucepan that is big enough to put a 1.5 litre hot-pot inside the saucepan for steaming. With the saucepan ⅓ full of the water, put the steaming rack inside.

- Before boiling the water for steaming, put all the ingredients inside the hot-pot, and add a litre of boiling water. Cover the top of the hot-pot with a large piece of grease proof paper, using a string to tie the paper in place, then cover the hot-pot lid tightly.

- Place the hot-pot inside the large saucepan on the steaming rack and cover the saucepan. Bring the water to the boil in a high heat, then reduce to moderate heat and steam for 4 hours. Check the saucepan regularly and add more boiling water if necessary.

- After 4 hours, remove the hot pot from the steamer. Take care not to spill the soup, open the lid of the hotpot and remove the string and grease paper. serves the soup in individual bowls.

*Useful tips:* *Covering the hot-pot with the grease proof paper is to prevent vapourised water adding into the soup during long period of steaming. It is also to seal the flavour within the soup.*

# Steamed Ching Po Liang Soup

Ching Po Liang is a classic Cantonese soup that can be prepared either savoury or sweet. Adding herbal ingredients to soup is very common in Cantonese cuisine. It is so common that you can get the ingredients readily packaged and sold in Chinese supermarkets; buying such a soup base pack is far cheaper than buying all the ingredients separately. This clear soup recipe only uses 4 main herbal ingredients.

## Serves 4

## Ingredient
150g pork cheek meat
40g dried lotus seeds
30g dried longan
20g Sa Sum (Adenophora)
20g Yuk Juck (also called jade bamboo, polygonatum odoratum)
600ml water
⅓ teaspoon salt

## Method

■ Wash all the ingredients, drain off excess water. Cut the pork cheek into 3 pieces.

■ Use a very large saucepan that is big enough to put a 1.5 litre hot-pot inside the saucepan for steaming. With the saucepan ⅓ full of the water, put the teaming rack inside.

■ Before boiling the water for steaming, put all the ingredients inside the hot-pot and add 600ml of boiling water into the pot. Cover the top of the hot-pot with a large piece of grease proof paper, using a string to tie the paper in place, then cover the hot-pot lid tightly.

■ Place the hot-pot inside the large saucepan on the steaming rack and cover the saucepan. Bring to boil on a high heat, then reduce to moderate heat and steam for 4 hours. Check the saucepan regularly and add more boiling water if necessary.

■ After 4 hours, remove the hot pot from the steamer. Take care not to spill the soup, open the lid of the hotpot and remove the string and grease paper. serves the soup in individual bowls.

*Useful tips:* You can use any lean pork meat for this soup. Pork cheek is a cheaper cut meat than any other part of the pork meat to use in cooking soup.

家禽

# Main Course - Poultry

# Chicken Fillet with Lemon Honey Sauce

Lemon chicken is a traditional Cantonese dish. Instead of deep-frying in batter, this recipe uses a lighter coating of bread crumbs. With a little creative flair plating the dish, you can serve this dish to impress any discerning guests.

## Serves 2-3

### Ingredient

500g boneless chicken breasts
1 unwaxed lemon, slightly grated the skin to remove the bitterness, sliced thinly and remove all the pips, keep them aside

### Seasoning

3 tablespoons cornflour
1 medium egg beaten

### Sauce

2 tablespoons cornflour
2 tablespoons concentrated lemon juice
1 tablespoon white rice wine vinegar
2 tablespoons water
4 tablespoons sugar

## Method

- Prepare the sauce ahead of cooking the chicken. Put all the sauce ingredients in a saucepan. Use a moderate heat to bring the liquid to boiling point then lower the heat and simmer the sauce, stirring all the time to prevent burning. When the sauce thickens, remove from the heat and leave aside to use later.

- Slice the chicken breasts through the thickest parts into halves to retain their shapes. Marinade the chicken evenly with corn flour and beaten egg. The coating at this stage should look sticky and glue - like.

- In an electric deep-fat fryer, use the recommended minimum volume of oil and heat to 220°C. Evenly coat the chicken with bread crumbs and deep-fry one piece a time until golden yellow. Remove from the fryer and drain off any excess oil on kitchen paper.

- To assemble the chicken, cut the chicken into 4cm x 4cm squares. Sandwich a slice of lemon between 2 pieces of chicken as illustrated.

- Warm up the sauce you prepared before and drizzle on the chicken. Serve immediately.

# Hong Kong Style Roast Duck

Hong Kong style roast duck is probably the most popular dish in Cantonese cuisine. Any restaurant that serves roast duck would also sell roast Cha siu and crispy roasted pork belly. These three delicacies will be proudly displayed to attract customers. Few of us would resist these temptations!

Traditionally, the ducks are best roasted in a hung oven, but nowadays, most fan assisted ovens are hot enough to roast an equally delicious roast duck at home.

## Serves 6-7

### Ingredient
1 fresh whole duck not less than 1.5kg

### 1st Seasoning
1 tablespoon salt
1 teaspoon sugar
1 tablespoon 5 spices
1 tablespoon oyster sauce
1 tablespoon light soy sauce
2 stalks of spring onion
50g peeled ginger crushed with a meat cleaver
3 star anise

### 2nd Seasoning
1 cup white rice vinegar
3 tablespoons of maltose syrup or golden syrup

## Method
- Mixed all the 1st seasoning ingredients in a bowl. Rub the mixture inside the duck cavity wall, tie the two leg nuckles together with a string to close the opening.

- Store in the refrigerator for 4 hours.

- After 4 hours, boil 2 litres of water in a wok. Place the duck into the boiling water for 1 minute. This technique is to remove the fats from the outer skin of the duck.

- Remove the duck from water and dry it with kitchen paper towel. Warm the vinegar and maltose syrup in a small saucepan and dilute the syrup completely without boiling the liquid.

- Use a kitchen brush to glaze the duck surface with the vinegar liquid. Repeat few times to get as much syrup on the duck as possible.

- If possible, have the duck hung openly and let the liquid drain out from the cavity. When all the liquid drain out, use a large mixing bowl and place a steaming rack at the bottom of the bowl. Stands the duck upward and store in the refrigerator for at least 6 hours.

- Preheat the oven to 200°C. Place the duck on a roasting rack inside a large roasting tin. Roast the duck on the lower rack for 30 minutes, turn the duck and roast for a further 40 minutes.

- Stand the roasted duck for 20 minutes after roasting. Cut in portions or bite-size pieces. Serve immediately.

# Kung Po Chicken

Kung Po chicken is a traditional Szechuan dish. The tender succulent boneless chicken pieces and the crunchiness of cucumber and peppers, combine a range of hot spicy, sweet and sour tastes to whet your appetite. Adding fried peanuts is a must in this dish.

## Serves 3-4

### Ingredients

150g boneless leg of chicken
75g cucumber
15g dried whole Szechuan chillies
50g green and red peppers
25g shelled peanuts
2 cloves of finely chopped garlic

### Seasoning

2 tablespoons vegetable cooking oil
⅓ teaspoon salt
½ teaspoon sugar
1 tablespoon white rice vinegar

### Thickening

1 teaspoon corn flour
3 tablespoons water

## Method

■ Cut the chicken meat into approximately 1.5cm cubes.

■ Without peeling the skin from the cucumber. Slice the cucumber lengthways into 2 halves, remove the seeds from both halves. Cut the cucumber into 1.5cm cubes and set aside. Cut the green and red peppers to a similar size.

■ Heat a wok or frying pan to a moderate heat. Using 2 tablespoons vegetable cooking oil swirl around the wok. Put all the peanuts into the wok - fry on a low heat, stirring all the time to prevent burning. This will take 5-7 minutes. Remove from the wok when the peanuts look light brown in colour. Set aside to use later.

■ Reheat the wok to high temperature and using the same oil you fried the peanuts earlier, pour in all the chopped garlic and dry red chillies and stir-fry for 10 seconds. Add the chicken to the wok and glaze for 1 minute. Then add all the green and red pepers, and cucumber, into the wok and stir-fry for 2 minutes. Blend in salt, sugar and vinegar for another minute.

■ Before serving, mix the corn flour with water and pour the liquid into the wok and stir until the sauce thickens. Add the fried peanuts and stir once or twice. Serve immediately.

*Useful tip: You can omit the peanuts in this recipe if you know someone in your family has nuts allergy. Szechuan chillies should be cooked in whole for its fragrant, not to be eaten unless you like your food fiery hot.*

# Roasted Duck in Plum Sauce

It is a Cantonese tradition to eat roast duck with plum sauce. However, if you have any left- over's from a previous recipe, you can transform your left-over roast duck into a Cantonese classic. If you don't have left-over's, ready cooked roast ducks are available in most Chinese supermarkets.

## Serves 1-2

### Ingredients
A quarter of Roast Duck (1 portion)

### Seasoning
3 tablespoons plum sauce

## Method

- If you use ready cooked roasted duck, it is best to have the duck cut into pieces first.

- Place the duck meat skin-side down in a wok or frying pan. Using a low heat to warm up the duck for approximately 2 minutes. Turn the meat over to warm for a further 2 minutes.

- Add 3 tablespoons of plum sauce over the duck. Turn the heat off when the sauce is bubbling. Serve at once.

- If you are serving your home-made roast duck with the plum sauce. Try to warm up the sauce in a small sauce pan. When the sauce is bubbling, drizzle over the roasted duck.

# Braised Chicken Wings in Cola sauce

This is a dish where the East meets the West. Adding cola into cooking is common in the Deep South of America. Adopting the idea into oriental cooking, the sweetness and spikiness of the cola taste, makes this dish a favourite amongst the old and young.

## Serves 1-2

### Ingredients
6 pieces middle part chicken wing
1 cup of cola
½ teaspoon sesame seeds

### Seasoning
1 tablespoon vegetable cooking oil
1 teaspoon cornflour (for thickening)
3 tablespoons water (for thickening)

### Condiments
Fried potato chips

## Method
- Clean the chicken wings and dried them with kitchen paper towel.

- Heat the wok or frying pan to moderate heat. Pour in a tablespoon of vegetable cooking oil and swirling this around the wok. Place the chicken wings in the wok/pan-fry until both sides are golden brown (approximately 5 minutes).

- Add the cola to the wok and cook for a further 5 minutes until half of the liquid evaporated. Mix the corn flour with 3 tablespoons of water and blend in the chicken to cook until the sauce has thickened. Stir well and then add the sesame seeds.

- Served with fried potato chips.

*Useful tip:* Do not use diet or zero cola to cook this dish, the sweetener used in these cola gives a bitter taste after cooking.

# Deep Fried Chicken

Also known as "Red Fried Chicken", one of the few must have roasting dishes for a Cantonese banquet. The key secret of the Deep Red fried chicken is the different stages of the cooking process. The result is a tasty chicken with an outer crispy skin yet a tender and moist inner.

## Serves 3-4

### Ingredients
1 small organic chicken (approx. 1kg in weight) make sure the chicken skin is not torn in any part.
2 litres vegetable cooking oil

### 1st Seasoning
3 tablespoons salt
2 teaspoons 5 spice powder
2 teaspoons shajiang powder (Kaempferiae galangae)

### 2nd Seasoning
½ cup of white rice wine vinegar
1½ tablespoon Maltose

### Condiments
lettuce leaves
Prawn crackers

*Note:* Maltose is a treacle like sugar made from wheat starch, available in most Chinese supermarket.

*Useful tip: If preferred, you can roast the chicken in an oven, preheat the oven to 190°c (180°c if using a fan assist oven), use a roasting tin, place the chicken onto a roasting rack bone-side down, roast for 30 minutes.*

## Method
- Mixed all the 1st seasoning ingredients, rub the seasoning generously inside and outside of the chicken. Covered the chicken with cling film and keep refrigerated for 2 hours.

- Warm up the white rice wine vinegar in a saucepan and add the maltose. Stir until the maltose completely dissolved. Keep aside for the 2nd seasoning.

- After 2 hours, use a large saucepan to boil 2 litres of water. Boil the marinated chicken for 2 minutes - the chicken is not expected to be thoroughly cooked at this stage. Remove the chicken and dry it with kitchen paper towel.

- When cooled, wipe the chicken with paper towel to remove excess liquid or jelly. Use a kitchen brush to brush every part of the chicken skin with the syrup-vinegar; brush on as much syrup as possible.

- The next stage is to "hang" the chicken. Use a large mixing bowl, place a round metal steam steaming rack in the bowl, stand the bottom part of the chicken onto the rack and cover loosely with cling film. Store in the refrigerator for 3-4 hours.

- In an electric deep-fryer, heat the oil to 150°C. Depends on the capacity of your fryer, you can either put the whole chicken in the fryer to deep-fry for 25 minutes, or cut in 2 halves to fry one at a time for 20 minutes each.

- Drain off any excess oil from the chicken. When it is cool enough to cut, use a meat cleaver and clean chopping board to cut the chicken into bite-size pieces. Arrange in a serving dish and served with lettuce leaves and prawn crackers.

# Soy Sauce Chicken

If you have been tempted by the roasted duck and pork, you may also tempted to try this delicious chicken that cooked in soy sauce. This Cantonese classic dish is made easyly by using the ready mixed ingredients available in Chinese supermarket. By adding light and dark soy sauces, an aromatic and succulent chicken will be ready in 30 minutes. You can reused the sauce to cook chciken again next time, or use the sauce in your other cooking.

## Serves 3-4

### Ingredients

1 organic chicken approximately 1.5kg in weight

### Sauce

30g ready mixed dried spices for soy sauce chicken
60ml light soy sauce
40ml dark soy sauce
3 tablespoon sugar
1 litre water

*Note:* The ready mixed spices containing, dried ginger, star anise, cinnamon, fennel seeds and Szechuan peppercorn

## Method

- Put all the sauce ingredients into a large pot. Bring to the boil and then lower the heat to simmer for 30 minutes.

- Wash the chicken and dry with kitchen towels.

- Put the chicken into the simmering liquid and keep on a low heat to simmer for a further 30 minutes.

- Drain all the liquid and remove any spices from the chicken. Let the chicken stands for 20 minutes before cutting it to small pieces.

- Use a tablespoon to remove excess oil from the sauce. Drizzle the sauce over the chicken when served.

- Once the sauce cool down, pour it in a glass jar or plastic box to store in the freezer for future use.

# Sweet & Sour Chicken

Adding sweet and sour to cooking is a popular method in Hunan cuisine, which is in Northeast China. This Cantonese version is less spicy and very easy to make.

## Serves 2

### Ingredients

200g skinless, boneless chicken breasts
4 tablespoons corn flour
1 medium egg
500ml vegetable cooking oil
10 pieces fresh or tin pineapple
1 quarter of green and 1 quarter red
   peppers, deseeded and cut into
   3X3cm pieces
1 small carrot cut into 1cm pieces

### Sauce

40ml white rice wine vinegar
3 tablespoons sugar
2 tablespoon tomato puree

## Method

■ Cut chicken breast to 2.5 X 2.5cm pieces.

■ Use 1 beaten egg to marinade the chicken and add 4 tablespoons corn flour to mix in with the chicken.

■ Preheat the deep-fat fryer to the meat setting with the minimum amount of oil recommended by the manufacturer. When at temperature, start to fry the chicken one piece at a time in the fryer. Fry the chicken until golden brown, remove from fryer and drain excess oil on kitchen towel.

■ Heat a wok or frying pan to a moderate heat and add 2 tablespoons of vegetable cooking oil. Add the green and red peppers, pineapple and carrot to stir-fry in the wok for 3 minutes. Add all the sauce ingredients into the wok and simmer. Add the fried chicken into the sauce and continue to stir the sauce all the time until the liquid has evaporated. Remove from the wok and serve immediately.

# Spicy Deep-fried Chicken

This is a classic Szechuan dish, famed for the bold flavours, particularly the spiciness resulting from the liberal use of chillies Szechuan peppercorns give the dish a fragrant, numbing, and citrusy flavour. This dish can also be prepared by steaming or braising.

## Serves 2-3

### Ingredients

Half chicken (approximately 400g)
10-12 dried whole Szechuan chillies
1 tablespoon Szechuan peppercorns
1 litre vegetable cooking oil for frying

### Marinade

½ teaspoon chilli powder
½ teaspoon salt
½ teaspoon sugar
½ teaspoon chicken powder
2 tablespoons cornflour

### Sauce

½ teaspoon salt
½ teaspoon sugar
1 large clove garlic crushed
1 spring onion finely chopped
2 tablespoons vegetable cooking oil
1 tablespoon light soy sauce
3 tablespoons water

## Method

- Cut chicken into 3 X 3cm pieces.

- Use all the marinade ingredients to marinade the chicken.

- In an electric deep-fryer, heat the oil to the meat setting with the recommended minimum volume of oil necessary. When the oil is heated, start to fry the chicken one at a time in the fryer. Fry the chicken until it is golden brown. Remove from fryer and drain off excess oil on kitchen paper towel.

- Heat a clean wok to very high heat and pour 2 tablespoons of oil into the wok. Add the crushed garlic, dried chillies and Szechuan peppercorns and stir-fry for 30 seconds. Add the chicken into the wok and mix all the ingredients evenly. Then add the salt, sugar, light soy sauce and water and stir vigorously until the liquid has evaporated.

- Turn off the heat and the dish is ready to serve.

海鮮

菜譜

*Bong Lam.*

# Main Course - Seafood

# Aubergine Towers

This is a modern Cantonese dish, with a fusion of seafood sandwiched between aubergine slices, combining the taste of prawn, scallop and squid with the creaminess of the aubergine in one bite. A truly delightful dish to whet your appetite.

## Serves 1-2

### Ingredients

1 large aubergine (at least 7cm diameter)
50g uncooked prawns
50g fresh or frozen scallops
50g fresh squid
50g red and green peppers
1 clove of garlic finely chopped
2 slices of ginger finely chopped

### Seasoning

½ teaspoon (2g) salt
½ teaspoon (2g) sugar
1 tablespoon vegetable cooking oil
1 tablespoon light soy sauce
1 teaspoon cornflour
5 tablespoons water

*Useful tip: you can deep fry the aubergine slices in a deep-fryer instead of frying them in a wok or frying pan, aubergine absorbs more oil during frying, but release the oil after they are cooked.*

## Method

- Remove shells from the prawns. Clean and dry the prawns, scallops and squid. Cut 2 pieces of prawn in half and leave 2 pieces of scallop uncut - dice the rest of the seafood into approximately 1cm pieces.

- Dice the green and red peppers to similar size.

- Mix all the seasoning ingredients in a bowl with 5 tablespoons of water, leave this aside to use later.

- Heat a wok or a large frying pan to a high heat with 10-12 tablespoons cooking oil.

- Discard the top and bottom of the aubergine and cut 6 (2.5cm thick) slices. Place immediately into the oil and fry each side until soft and golden brown. Remove from the wok and keep them aside for assemble later.

- Pour out excess oil from the wok or frying pan and reheat to very hot until smoke rises. Put the chopped garlic and ginger into the wok and stir for 10 seconds. Then put all the diced seafood and peppers into the wok and stir-fry rapidly for 3 minutes. Stir all the mixed seasonings to prevent the corn flour sticking to the bottom. Pour the mixed ingredients into the wok and blend in with the seafood and peppers for 1 minute. Turn off the heat and you are ready to assemble the tower.

- Place 2 slices of fried aubergine on a serving dish. Using a tablespoon, generously scoop the mixed seafood and peppers on top of the aubergines. Continue the process until 3 layers have been built. Decorate the top layers with the large pieces of prawn and the whole scallops. Pour any remaining sauce on top of each tower and serve immediately.

# Pan Fried Fish with Hot & Spicy Sauce

Pan fried fish with hot and spicy sauce is a delicious dish cooked simply to bring out the natural favours of the fish. The dish is threaded with the numbing spicy heat from the sauce yet it is also quick and simple to make.

## Serves 2-3

### Ingredients
400g boneless fillet of fish
1 medium egg
3 tablespoon vegetable cooking oil

### Seasoning
2 tablespoons cornflour
¼ teaspoon sesame seeds oil
¼ teaspoon ground white peppers

### Sauce
½ teaspoon chilli powder
3 teaspoons sugar
2 tablespoons tomato puree
2½ tablespoons water

### Condiments
Fresh red chilli cut finely in rings
Spring onions cut finely in strips

## Method

- Cut the fish fillets into 5cm X 3cm pieces.

- Add ground peppers, sesame oil and beaten egg to marinade the fish.

- Prepare the corn flour in a large dish.

- Heat the wok or frying pan to very high heat, add 3 tablespoons of oil in the wok and swirl around.

- Coat the marinated fish fillets lightly with the corn flour. Then place the fish into the wok to fry for 2 minutes on each side. Taking care not to break the fish when you turn them during frying.

- You can either arrange the fish fillets away from the centre of the wok to give room for making sauce, or place the cooked fish fillets on a serving dish. Add all the chillies into the wok to fry for 30 seconds. Add all the sauce ingredients to the wok to cook for another 30 seconds.

- Pour sauce over the fish and serve.

# Poached Fish Fillets in Hot Chilli Oil

Poached fish with added dried chillies and Szechuan peppercorns are a typical Szechuan speciality. the added spices are for the distinctive aroma release into the fish when cooked. It is not necessary to eat the chilli and peppercorns, unless you are used to the heat.

Tou Ban sauce is used in this recipe, this sauce is originally from Szechuan, made with yellow beans and rolled oats. Tou Ban sauce has a distinctive taste, different to it's southern cousin - soy bean paste. It is best used in fish or mince pork dishes.

## Serves 2-3

### Ingredients

400g skinless and boneless fillet of fish
Large handful of bean sprouts
20 dried red chillies
3 spring onion cut into 5 cm pieces and then cut into half vertically

### Marinade

¼ teaspoon salt
¼ teaspoon sesame seeds oil
¼ teaspoon ground white peppers
I egg white
I tablespoon corn flour

### Sauce

I teaspoon Tou Ban sauce
2 tablespoons oil
2½ tablespoons water
½ teaspoon sesame oil

### Condiments

1-2 stalks coriander

## Method

- Cut the fish fillets into 3cm thick slices.

- Carefully blend in all the marinade ingredients and add to the fish. Set the fish aside in the marinade.

- Heat a wok to a moderate heat and pour 2 tablespoons of vegetable cooking oil into the wok. Wait until smoke rises and add the Touban sauce to the oil and stir vigorously for 20 seconds. Then add the bean sprouts to stir-fry with the sauce for 1 minute. Turn the heat off and lay the fried bean sprouts in a large serving dish.

- In the same wok, add 2½ tablespoons of water and bring to boil. Add the marinated fish to the wok. Covered with lid and cook for 2 minutes. Place the fish on top of the bean sprouts in the serving dish.

- Clean the wok and heat it up to a moderate heat. Add the dried red chillies, peppercorns and spring onion to the wok and stir-fry for 30 seconds. Turn off the heat and drizzle the spices on top of the fish. Garnish with coriander and serve immediately.

# Braised Sardine in Black Bean Sauce

This is another traditional Cantonese dish. Canton (now called Guangdong) is situated by the South China Sea with more than 4,300km of coastline. Cantonese cuisine has more seafood dishes than any other regional cuisines. The natives use local fished herrings to cook this dish. In this recipe we used sardines as a substitute.

## Serves 3-4

### Ingredients

3-4 large sardines, scaled, remove guts and head.
4 tablespoons vegetable cooking oil

### Seasoning

2 tablespoons Yangjiang fermented black beans
2 large cloves of garlic, peel and crushed finely
1 medium hot green chilli deseeded and roughly chopped)
1 medium hot red chilli deseeded and roughly chopped)
1 tablespoon light soy sauce
1 tablespoon oyster sauce
1 tablespoon rice cooking wine
½ teaspoon salt
½ teaspoon sugar
½ cup of water

## Method

- Scored each side of the fish 5 times to help with the absorbtion of the sauce and firm up the fish.

- Washed the fermented black beans. Using the back of a tablespoon, mash the beans slightly. Mixed the finely crushed garlic and the roughly chopped chillies and marinade the fish on both inside and the outside.

- Heat a wok or frying pan to very high heat until smoke rises. When ready pour the oil in and swirl around the wok. Fry both sides of the fish until golden brown. Add the remaining seasoning ingredients into the wok to braise the fish. Covered with a lid for 5 minutes.

- Serve the fish with rice.

# Salt and Pepper King Prawns

Green and red peppers are used in this classic Cantonese dish to add the colour to the prawns. Combining onion, garlic and aromatic red chilli, this makes the perfect dish for any dinner party.

## Serves 3-4

### Ingredients

8 large king prawns
1 medium egg yolk
20g green and red peppers
½ onion finely chopped
1 medium hot red chilli
½ litre of vegetable cooking oil

### Seasoning

1 tablespoons chilli oil
1 teaspoon salt
4 tablespoons cornflour

## Method

■ Remove the shells from the prawns but keep the tails. Remove the veins by cutting the back of the prawns and slightly opening them and gently pulling to remove the vein. Clean and dry the prawns.

■ Cut the green and red peppers into small pieces. De-seed the red chillis by cutting away the top and then removing the seeds with a small sharp knife. Cut the chilli's in small rings.

■ Crack an egg and drain out the egg white. Beat the egg yolk and blend into the prawns. Ensure the prawns are completely coated. Add salt and corn flour to the prawns and mix well.

■ Heat the wok with ½ litre of oil in it. Test the oil temperature by dropping a small piece of bread into the oil. When the bread looks golden brown, the temperature should be hot enough. Put the prawns in to fry for 1 minute. Remove them soon after the prawns look golden yellow.

■ Remove the oil from wok into a metal measuring jug to cool.

■ Reheat the same wok and add 1 tablespoon of chilli oil. Add the onion, peppers and red chilli rings and stir-fry for 30 seconds. Mix the fried prawns into the wok and add salt. Toss the prawns with a wok spatula a few times. Turn off the heat and you are ready to serve.

# Salt and Pepper Squid

This dish is the same as the salt and pepper prawns recipe but you replace the prawns with fresh squid. This is also a classic Cantonese dish. The texture of the squid is slightly chewy if over-cooked; therefore, it is best to cook quickly in this recipe.

## Serves 3-4

## Ingredients

300g fresh squids
1 medium egg yolk
20g green and red peppers
½ onion finely chopped
1 medium hot red chilli
½ litre of vegetable cooking oil

## Seasoning

1 tablespoons chilli oil
1 teaspoon salt
4 tablespoons corn flour

## Method

- Remove the head and tentacles and the enclosed mantle masses from the body of the squid. Clean and dry the squid with kitchen paper towels.

- First prepare the body by cutting open one side of the squid vertically so that it is a flat piece. Use a sharp knife to score across the surface diagonally then score again vertically to give little squares patterns.

- Once you have finished scoring the squid, cut the squid into 4 long pieces. Then use the knife slice at an angle to cut the squid in 4-5cm pieces.

- Crack an egg and drain out the egg white and beat the egg yolk. Blend in the squid and ensure that the squid is completely coated with the egg. Add salt and corn flour to the squid - mix well.

- Heat the wok with ½ litre of oil. Test the oil temperature by dropping a small piece of bread into the oil. When the bread looks golden brown, the temperature should be hot enough. Put the squid in to fry for 1 minute. Be aware that the squid cooks very quickly. The scoring and slicing of the squid helps to cook the squid evenly. Remove the squid soon after they begin curling and looking golden yellow.

- Remove the oil from wok into a metal measuring jug to cool.

- Reheat the same wok and add 1 tablespoon of chilli oil. Add the onion, peppers and red chilli rings and stir-fry for 30 seconds. Mix the fried squid into the wok and add salt. Toss the squid with a wok spatula a few times. Turn off the heat your dish is ready to serve.

# Mussels in Black Bean Sauce

This is a traditional Cantonese coastal dish. Mussels taste particularly good with black bean sauce.

## Serves 3-4

### Ingredients
600g fresh mussels
3 tablespoons vegetable cooking oil

### Seasoning
2 tablespoons Yangjiang fermented black
  beans
1 teaspoon sugar
1 tablespoon oyster sauce
1 tablespoon light soy sauce
2 tablespoon water
2 cloves of garlic finely chopped
15g red and green chillies

### Thickening
1 teaspoon corn flour
3 tablespoons water

## Method

- In a big bowl of clean water, wash and brush the mussels and remove all the beards. Rinse and keep them to drain in a colander.

- Put all the cleaned mussels into a wok or large saucepan. Pour in enough water to just cover the mussels. Boil the water until all the mussel shells are opened. Once the shells have opened, any sand inside the mussels should be released into the water. Remove from the heat and drain the mussels in a colander.

- Wash the black beans and mash lightly with the back of a tablespoon.

- Clean and heat the wok to high heat. Pour 3 tablespoons of oil in and swirl around to coat the wok. Add the chopped garlic, chillies and black beans and stir in the oil for 20 seconds. Add all the mussels into the wok and then add the sugar, oyster sauce and water and stir-fry for 2 minutes.

- Before serving, add the diluted cornflour liquid into the wok and blend until the sauce thickens. Serve at once.

*Useful tips:* Do not use boiling water to blanch the mussels, using cold water to heat the water up with the mussels gradually will help the mussels to release the sands and open.

# Braised Lobster with Shredded Ginger and Spring Onion

Lobster is often served in Chinese banquets as the seafood course. Cooking lobster at home is much easier than you can imagine and much cheaper than it would be at a restaurant.

## Serves 1-2

### Ingredient
1 large lobster (approximately 900g)

### Seasoning
½ teaspoon salt
½ teaspoon sugar
50g onion
5 slices ginger, cut in thin strips
2 spring onion
3 cloves of garlic finely chopped
2 red chillies finely chopped
2 green chillies finely chopped
15ml Chinese rice wine
5 tablespoons vegetable cooking oil
80ml water
15g butter

### How to prepare a lobster
- Prepare a large saucepan of boiling water. Do make sure to wear a pair of rubber gloves, and have a brush with handle to clean the lobster.

- Put the lobster under a cold water tap and run cold water over it, brush the lobster.

- Put the lobster into the boiling water and cover with the lid for 30 seconds. This is the most humane way of killing a lobster. Remove the lobster from the boiling water and place under the tap and run cold water over it for 5 minutes.

## Method
- Carefully pull the head and claws away from the body. Use a small hammer or the back of a meat cleaver to crack the claws. Cut the body in half and then cut each half into 5 pieces. Keep them aside for cooking later.

- Cut the Spring onions into 5cm lengths. Then cut each piece in half vertically, and then cut them into thin strips vertically. Immerse all the strips in a bowl of cold water to make them curly. Leave them aside for later.

- Heat the wok to a high heat and pour 5 tablespoons of vegetable oil into the wok, then add the onion, garlic, ginger and chillies and fry for 30 seconds.

- Place all the lobster pieces into the wok and stir vigorously. Then add the salt, sugar and rice wine to blend into the lobster.

- Pour water into the wok and cover the wok with lid and simmer for 6 minutes.

- Remove the lid and add butter into the wok and mix well. Turn off the heat.

- In a large serving dish, arrange the lobster by putting the head to one side and the tail parts to the opposite side. Fill the center with the remaining lobster. Garnish the lobster with curly spring onion and serve immediately.

# Huadiao Steamed Queen Crab

In this recipe, Queen crabs (or snow crab) are chosen for their distinctive delicate taste. They are best eaten steamed with a little aged old 'Huadiao' (also called Huangjiu) Chinese rice wine. This is a traditional local wine of the Zhejiang province brewed with rice. Because the wines use different fermentation stater, it contains less than 20% alcohol. 'Huadiao' is commonly used in Chinese cooking to add extra favour to meat, poultry and seafood.

## Serves 2

### Ingredient

2 medium size live Queen crabs
30ml Huangjiu Chinese rice wine

### Sauce

3 tablespoons red rice vinegar
2 tablespoon light soy sauce

## How to prepare the crabs

- Prepare a large saucepan of boiling water,

- Before steaming the crabs, if they are alive, do make sure to wear a pair of rubber gloves and have a brush with handle to clean the crabs one at a time.

- Flip the crab on its back in the sink under a cold water tap and run cold water over it, brush the crab. This way, the crab will feel dizzy and struggle less. Once clean on one side, flip it over and brush the other side clean.

- Keep the clean crab on its back to prevent it crawling around. Now wash the second crab the same way as the first one.

- As soon as they are cleaned, dip them into the boiling water and cover the lid for 30 seconds. This is the most humane way of killing a crab. Remove the crabs from the boiling water and run cold water over them.

- Wait till the crabs are cool enough to work with. Firstly, pull the carapace away and then remove the flap from the abdomen. Remove the air gills and cut the crab from the middle of the abdomen.

- Place the crabs in a large bowl and pour the rice wine over the crab. Steam the crabs either in a wok or steamer for 15 minutes. Serve at once with red rice vinegar and light soy sauce as a dip.

# Steamed Egg with Crab roe

In this recipe, only the carapace of the crab is used for cooking. Therefore, blue crab is recommended for its size because it is large enough to hold the beaten egg for steaming. Live blue crabs are available at the fish counter of Chinese supermarkets or good local fish mongers. You can ask the fish monger to kill and clean the crab for you, however if you prefer to prepare the crab at home, please refer to the previous recipe instructions on "How to prepare the crabs".

## Serves 1

### Ingredient
1 large blue crab
1 medium egg
20ml water

### Seasoning
⅓ teaspoon salt
a dash of ground pepper
2-3 drops of sesame seed oil
½ spring onion finely chopped

## Method

- Use a tablespoon to scoop out the roe inside the crab carapace. Remove the air gills.

- Beaten one egg with 20ml water and add all the seasoning ingredients.

- Pour the egg mixture into the carapace; add the crab roe in the egg, spring over the chopped spring onion.

- Place the carapace inside the steamer carefully and steam for 12 minutes on a high heat. When the egg and crab roe mixture are set, serve immediately.

# Steamed Egg with Seafood

Ask any Chinese what is their children's favourite food and they would probably tell you this dish - Steamed egg with seafood. You can use any boneless and shell-less seafood in this recipe, because the presentation of this dish is very unusual and it makes an impressive dish to serve at a dinner party.

## Serves 3

### Ingredients

3 king prawns with shell
12 pieces of seafood stick
or 1 tub of crab meat
4 medium free-range eggs
400ml water
few sprigs of chives finely chopped

### Seasoning

½ teaspoon salt

## Method

- Prepare 3 heat resistant small bowls.

- Use crab meat or tear the seafood sticks into thin strips. Keep 12 thin strips aside for garnishing later. Divide the rest fill in each bowl. Remove the shells from the prawns, but keep the tails. stand each prawn tail side up in the middle of the bowl.

- Beat 4 eggs and add water and salt to beat thoroughly. Fill each bow with the same volume of the egg mixture.

- Fill a steamer to a ⅓ full of boiling water. Place the bowls inside the perforated pan and stack the pan on top of the steamer.

- Covered the steamer with a lid and steam the egg in high heat for 15 minutes.

- Before serving, garnish 4 strips of seafood and the chopped chives on top of each bowl and serve at once.

# Steamed Sea Bass fillet

Fish is one of the main types of seafood eaten by Chinese. Steaming is far more common than any other cooking method. In this recipe, sea bass is chosen for its delicate texture and taste.

## Serves 1-2

### Ingredient

1 large sea bass (approximately 400g) filleted

### Seasoning

2 tablespoons light soy sauce
2 tablespoons vegetable cooking oil
5 large slices of ginger
5 spring onions
1 medium hot red chilli

## Method

- Close the sea bass fillets together with the skin side facing top and bottom. Carefully cut the double fillets into 4X4 cm squares.

- Cut the ginger slices into thin strips. De-seed the red chilli and cut the chilli into thin strips similar to the ginger. Discard the lower green part of the spring onions and cut the rest into 5cm lengths. Then cut each piece in half vertically, and then cut each half into small strip vertically. Immerse all the spring onion strips in a bowl of cold water to make the strips curly. Leave these aside for later.

- Fill the wok a ⅓ full of boiling water and place a steaming rack into the water and stand the plate on the rack. Ensure the water level is only reaching half way up the rack.

- Covered the wok with a lid and steam the fish on a high heat for 10 minutes.

- While steaming the fish, use a small saucepan to heat up 2 tablespoons of oil and 2 tablespoons of light soy sauce. Before serving the fish, garnish the fish with ginger, red chilli and curly spring onion strips on top of each square. Drizzle the oil and soy sauce mixture onto the fish and serve immediately.

# Steamed Garlic King Prawns

Steamed prawns is common in Chinese cuisine. Different regions add different ingredients. This version is one of the classic dishes often served at Chinese banquets. It is very simple to make and the outcome is very tasty.

## Serves 3

### Ingredients
6 large king prawns (approximately 200g)

### Seasoning
3 cloves garlic, crushed and very finely chopped
1 spring onion, finely chopped
3 tablespoon vegetable cooking oil

### Sauce
2 tablespoons vegetable cooking oil
2 tablespoons light soy sauce

## Method
- Washed and dried the prawns with kitchen paper towels.

- Prepare an oblong plate for laying the prawns as illustrated.

- Using a pair of scissors, trim off the long beards and gills from the head, trimming off the gills under the body.

- Cut off the head from each prawn with a sharp knife and stand them at the long edge of the plate upward. Without removing the shell, use the sharp knife to cut into the shell at the back of the prawns. Cut into the meat half way and force the prawn to open slightly.

- Mixed chopped garlic, spring onion and oil together. Fill the open cavity with the mixture to form a heap at the back of the prawns.

- Fill the wok with a ⅓ full of boiling water and place a steaming rack in the water and stand the plate on the rack. Ensure the water level is only reaching half way of the rack.

- Covered the wok with a lid and steam the prawns on a high heat for 1 minute.

- While steaming the prawns. Use a small saucepan to heat up 2 tablespoons of oil and 2 tablespoons of light soy sauce. When the prawns are ready, drizzle the oil and soy sauce mixture onto the prawns and serve immediately.

# Deep Fried Mayo King Prawns

There are many versions of deep fried king prawns. This one uses light bread crumbs coating to retain the moisture in the prawns and drizzled with mayonnaise sauce.

## Serves 1-2

## Ingredients
8 large uncook king prawns
20g breadcrumbs
1 medium egg
½ teaspoon sesame seeds
1 litre vegetable cooking oil (for frying)

## Seasoning
2 teaspoons cornflour
4 tablespoons mayonnaise
⅓ teaspoon salt

## Method
■ Clean the prawns after removing shells and de-vein them.

■ Preheat the deep-fryer to 200°C or fish setting.

■ Add salt to season the uncook prawns and add a little beaten egg to coat the prawns. Sprinkle the corn flour on top and mix to a slightly wet texture. Add more egg if it is too dry.

■ Put the breadcrumbs into a large dish and roll the prawns individually until they are completely covered with breadcrumbs.

■ In an electric deep-fry, heat the oil to the seafood setting. When the oil is ready, start to fry the prawns in the fryer, preferably one at a time to prevent lowering the oil temperature. Fry all the prawns until light golden brown, put them on a serving dish.

■ Drizzle the prawns with mayonnaise and sesame seeds and serve immediately.

*Useful tips:* Do not overcook the prawns, as this will result in prawns being chewy.

# Steamed Sea Bass fillet in Black Bean Sauce

This is an elaborate version of steamed sea bass with black bean sauce. This dish often served as one of the seafood dishes during Chinese banquet. Sea bass is chosen not only for it's delicate texture and taste, but also chosen for its presentation.

## Serves 3-4

### Ingredient

1 large sea bass (approximately 400g) filleted, keep the head
5 spring onions

### Seasoning

5 large slices of ginger, cut the slices into thin strips
2 tablespoons Yangjiang fermented black beans
1 tablespoon oyster sauce
1 medium hot red chilli, cut into thin strips

### Sauce

1 tablespoons light soy sauce
½ teaspoon sesame seed oil
2 tablespoons vegetable cooking oil

### Condiments

Small pack of mixed curly leaves green salad
3 red baby tomatoes
3 yellow baby tomatoes

## Method

- Washed the black beans, using the back of a tablespoon to mash the beans slightly. Mixed in with all the seasoning ingredients

- Closed the sea bass fillets together with the skin side facing top and bottom. Carefully cut the double fillets into 4X4 cm squares. Arrange the fillets in a round dish as illustrated and insert a red baby tomato into the fish mouth. Spoon the mixed seasoning on top of each fillet square.

- Cut the spring onions into 5cm lengths, then cut each piece vertically in thin strip. Immerse all the spring onion into a bowl of cold water to make the strips curly. leave them aside for later.

- Fill the wok to a ⅓ full of boiling water and place a steaming rack in the water and stand the plate on the rack. Ensure water level is only reaches half way up the rack.

- Covered the wok with a lid and steam the fish on a high heat for 10 minutes.

- While steaming the fish, use a small saucepan to heat up all the sauce ingredients. Before serving the fish, garnish the fish with curly spring onion strips on top of each square. Garnish the green salad and tomatoes in the middle on the dish. Drizzle the oil and soy sauce mixture onto the fish and salad. Serve immediately.

*Useful tips:* It is relatively easy to fillet a sea bass at home. Use a sharp fillet knife, insert into the fish below the head, holding your knife at an angle to make an incision, and then insert the knife over the back gills from top to slice down until the tail part. Holding the half filleted part of the fish with one hand and carry on using the fillet knife to separate the stomach of the fish away from the bones. Work in the same way on the other side of the fish.

# Main Course - Meat

# Garlic Crusty Spare Ribs

Garlic crusty spare ribs is a traditional Cantonese dish, the garlic flavoured crust is light and crunchy, whilst the meat is very tender when you bite into it.

## Serves 1-2

## Ingredients
600g pork spare ribs

## Seasoning
150g gluten rice flour
10g dried bread crumbs
2 teaspoons sugar
½ teaspoon chicken powder
½ teaspoon salt
250g peeled garlic
250ml water
1 medium egg (beaten)

## Condiments
100g thinly sliced peeled garlic

*Useful tip:* Do not over marinaded the spare ribs. After 2 hours, the natural chemical change of the crushed garlic causes bitter taste to the spare ribs.

## Method

- Use a meat cleaver to cut the spare ribs into roughly 6cm long pieces. Use a garlic presser to press all 250g peeled garlic into 250ml water.

- In a large food bag, put the spare ribs, pressed garlic and water - mix well. Seal the bag tighly, then transfer the bag into a food box with its lid tighly covered - this is to prevent the smell of raw garlic permeatinh into other food in your refrigerator. Marinade the spare ribs for 2 hours.

- Beat an egg in a dish. Use a separate dish for gluten rice flour and the bread crumbs. Remove the spare ribs from refrigerator and discard the liquid. Wash the spare ribs well, and dry with kitchen paper towel. Use the salt, sugar and chicken powder to rub in to the spare ribs. Dust the spare ribs with gluten rice flour.

- Set the electric deep-fryer to 200°C, when the oil is heated, start to prepare the spare ribs for frying.

- Completely coat all the spare ribs in beaten egg, but thinly. Transfer them into the gluten rice flour to cover the egg coating. Put the ribs back into the beaten egg for a second coat. Using a pair of chopsticks, take out the spare ribs and transfer them into the bread crumbs and coat completely.

- First fry the thinly sliced garlic, remove quickly to avoid burning, drain off any excess oil.

- Reduce the fryer's heat down to 150°C, place all the spare ribs into the fryer, turning them occasionally. Cook for 10 minutes or until golden brown.

- Drain off excess oil from spare ribs and put them ina serving dish. Spread the fried garlic on top and serve immediately.

# Beef Curry

Curry beef is a traditional Malaysian dish. There is a large population of ethnic Chinese living in Malaysia. When this dish introduced to mainland China, an idea came from tranforming a traditional Malaysian dish which evolved into a popular Cantonese favourite.

## Serves 5

### Ingredients
250g topside of beef or steak
2 medium size potatoes
2 tablespoons of frozen peas (defrosted)
A quarter each of green and red pepper

### Seasoning
1 teaspoon salt
1 beef stock cube
1 teaspoon sugar

### Sauce
1 tablespoon green curry powder
1 tablespoon plain flour
2-3 pieces of star anise
2 bay leaves
½ cinnamon stick
2 lemon grass stalks crush slightly with
   a meat cleaver
1 medium size onion
1 shallot finely chopped
1 clove of crushed garlic
1 crushed birdeye chilli (optional)
300ml of water

### Condiments
Lettuce leaves
Few slices of French bread

## Method

- Dice the beef, potato, green, red peppers and onion to 2cm squares. Keep all ingredients separate.

- First prepare the curry sauce, pour 3 tablespoons vegetable cooking oil into a wok or heavy-base sauce pan. On a medium heat, fry the onion, shallot and garlic. Then add the curry powder, star anise, bay leaves, cinnamon and lemon grass. Stir vigorously to prevent burning. Add seasoning according to taste. Dilute the pain flour with 300ml water, stir well until lumps disappear. Blend the liquid in the wok or saucepan for few second until the sauce has thickened.

- Put the cut beef and potato chunks into the sauce to cook. Turn the heat down to moderate and keep stirring to prevent the sauce from burning. Add the peas, green and red peppers to the wok and cook for a further 3 minutes.

- Before serving, remove the star anise and lemon grass from wok. Served with rice or French bread

*Useful tip: Unlike Indian curry, this curry recipe uses less spices to make, you can add chilli according to your taste.*

# Ma Poh Tofu

Ma Poh Tofu is another traditional Szechuan dish dating back to Qing Dynasty. The dish is named after a female restaurant vendor called Ma Poh who created this tofu dish cooked with minced pork. Ma Poh tofu is best served with boiled rice.

## Serves 2-3

## Ingredients
400g firm tofu
15g minced pork
18g green and red medium hot chillies
2 cloves of finely chopped garlic

## Seasoning
⅓ teaspoon salt
⅓ teaspoon sugar
½ chicken stock cube dilute in I cup (200ml) water
I teaspoon chilli powder
I tablespoon vegetable cooking oil
I teaspoon Szechuan peppercorns

## Thickening
I teaspoon cornflour
3 tablespoons water

## Method

- Dry the tofu with kitchen papper towel. Cut into 2cm cubes.

- Deseed the chillies by cutting the tops off and removing seeds. Cut them in 1cm rings and keep them aside to use later.

- Heat 1 tablespoon of vegetable cooking oil in a wok on high heat. Add the Szechuan peppercorns for 30 seconds to fragrance the oil. Remove them from the oil and discard them. Add the chopped garlic and fry for 20 seconds. Add the minced pork to the wok and stir-fry for 2 minutes.

- Add salt, sugar, chilli powder in the wok, and then carefully place all the tofu cubes into the wok. Use a spatula to turn the tofu gently to prevent the cubes from breaking.

- Covered the wok with a lid and cook for 1 minute. Before serving, blend the corn flour liquid into the wok, turning the tofu carefully until the sauce thickens. Serve imediately.

*Useful tips:* if the sauce is too thin, mix extra corn flour with little water then add to the sauce.

# Beef in Black Bean Sauce & Peppers

A favourite traditional Cantonese dish dating back to the Han Dynasty in Chinese culinary history. The dish uses the famous YangJiang local delicacy "fermented black bean", which is a well-guarded, century old, secret recipe, only known to local people.

Every chef concocts a black bean sauce differently. The distinctive pungent favour means you can use the same sauce to cook with any meat or seafood. This dish goes well with rice or noodles.

## Serves 2-3

### Ingredient

150g topside beef or steak
½ green pepper
½ red pepper
8g fermented black beans
2 cloves of garlic finely chopped
1 shallot

### Seasoning

3 tablespoons vegetable cooking oil
½ cup of water (125ml)
⅓ teaspoon salt
⅓ teaspoon beef stock cube
½ teaspoon sugar
1 teaspoon light soy sauce
2 drops of sesame seed oil
small pinch white ground pepper
Red or green chilli (optional)

### Thickening

1 teaspoon cornflour
3 tablespoon water

### Garnish

1 spring onion, finely chopped

## Method

- Wash the fermented black beans. Drain off the excess water with kitchen paper towel. Use the back of a tablespoon to mash the beans slightly and keep these aside. You can find ready made black bean sauces from any Chinese supermarket.

- Cut the beef into medium thin slices. Use 1 tablespoon of vegetable cooking oil and 2 drops of sesame seeds oil to marinade the sliced beef. Cut the green and red peppers to 3-4cm squares. Peel and slice the shallots to 1cm thick.

- Preheat the wok until it is very hot. Pour 2 tablespoons of cooking oil into the wok. Swirl the oil around the wok. Put the finely chopped garlic and shallots into the wok and fry for few seconds. Add the mashed black beans or ready made black bean sauce to the wok. Stir once or twice then put all the beef and peppers into the wok. Then add the rest of the seasoning ingredients to the wok - stir well and let it cook for 5 minutes.

- Before serving, add the chopped spring onion. Dilute the corn flour with water and blend in for few second until the sauce thickens. Then turn the heat off and serve in a serving dish.

# Roast Belly of Pork

One of the three traditional Cantonese roasted meats, a good roast belly of pork should have a crunchy, crackling skin and tender meat that almost melts in your month.

## Serves 4-5

## Ingredients

400g whole piece middle part of fresh
　pork belly

## 1st Seasoning

1 teaspoon 5 spices
1 tablespoon sugar
1 tablespoon Chu Hou sauce
2 tablespoons light soy sauce
1 tablespoon oyster sauce
1 teaspoon sesame seeds oil
½ teaspoon ground white pepper

## 2nd Seasoning

1½ cup white rice wine vinegar
3 tablespoons maltose

## Method

- Wipe the pork belly dry with kitchen paper towel. Use a skewer or the sharp end of the roasting meat thermometer, to pierce the whole of the pork skin vigorously.

- Mixed all of the first seasoning ingredients together and marinade the pork belly for 3 hours. After 3 hours rinse off all the first seasoning ingredients. wipe the pork belly dry.

- Whilst waiting for the pork belly skin to dry, prepare the second seasoning ingredients. Using a small saucepan to warm up the vinegar. Pour 3 tablepoons of maltose in the warm vinegar to dilute. Maltose is a treacle like sugar made from wheat starch which available in most Chinese supermarkets.

- Using a clean kitchen brush, brush the pork skin generously with the the maltose vinegar liquid. Cover the pork belly loosely with cling film and leave it out to dry for 3 hours. The first seasoning will have already preserved the meat. The drying process is important as this will helps with the breakdown of the meat so that it becomes very soft. The skin will begin to crackle during the roasting process.

- Preheat the oven to 200°C. With the skin side up, place the pork belly on a roasting rack and then stand this in a roasting tin which has 2 cups of water in it to catch the juice from meat during roasting. Roast the pork belly for 40 minutes without opening the oven door to check. It is important to keep the oven temperature constant during roasting.

- Remove the belly pork from the oven and stand the meat for 20 minutes before cutting in cubes and serving.

# Honey Roast Pork

Traditional Cantonese roasted meats; also called Cha-Siu. Using only the fillet of pork, the honey roast pork is one of the three roasted meats that often served as one dish. The tender roasted meat is best served with rice and is every child's favourite because the sweet taste of the meat.

## Serves 2-3

### Ingredients
400g pork fillet

### Seasoning
20g finely grated ginger
20g finely chopped onion
2 tablespoons light soy sauce
100g sugar
1 tablespoon honey
1 teaspoon salt

### Sauce
1 tablespoon honey

## Method

- Clean and wipe the pork fillet dry with kitchen paper towel. Mixed all the seasoning ingredients together and marinade the pork fillet for 2 hours.

- Preheat the oven to 190°C. Place the pork fillet into a roasting tin, roast the pork fillet for 35 minutes. Remove from oven, brush the roast pork with additional honey. Before serving, cut the roast por in bite size slices.

# Wor Bao Pork Fillet in Sweet & Sour Sauce

This is a classic dish from northeast China, the region neighbouring Russia in the north, and Korea in the east. It was the homeland of the Manchus, after conquering China and establishing the Qing dynasty. This is one of the many dishes often served at the Qing Imperial banquets.

## Serves 2

### Main Ingredient

300g fillet of pork
200ml vegetable cooking oil

### Seasoning

½ teaspoon salt
½ tablespoon rice cooking wine
1 tablespoon cornflour
2 tablespoons water

### Sauce

3 large slices ginger finely cut to thin strips
1 spring onion finely cut to thin strips
2 tablespoons tomato puree
1 tablespoon sugar
1 tablespoon dark rice vinegar
1 teaspoon sesame seeds

## Method

- Cut the pork fillet to 7mm thick slices. In a large bowl, add the seasoning ingredients to the meat and marinade. Ensure the liquid covers each piece of meat completely.

- Prepare the sauce in a small bowl. Add tomato puree, sugar and vinegar and keep to one side.

- Heat the oil in the deep-fryer to a moderate heat. You can test the heat by dripping a small piece of bread into the oil. When the bread turns to golden brown, the temperature should be hot enough to start frying the meat.

- Coat the meat evenly with the marinade and corn flour by mixing them in the bowl again. Carefully, place each piece into the oil to fry. Keep all the pieces separate and fry both sides until golden brown. Remove and drain off excess oil onto kitchen paper towel.

- When you have finished cooking the meat, pour the oil out in a bowl to cool, you can reuse the oil for cooking.

- Without adding oil in the wok/frying pan, add the thinly cut ginger strips in and stir-fry. Add the premixed sauce ingredients into the wok and simmer. When the sauce thickens (the sauce should not be runny), add the meat into wok and stir. Add the sesame seed and spring onion strips. This dish is now ready for serving.

*Useful tips:* *Try not to overcook the pork fillet when you fry them first time, if not sure, you can always test the first piece you cooked, its perfect if crunchy outside and moist inside without showing red in the meat.*

# Steamed Spare Ribs

In Cantonese cusine, many dishes are cooked in a steamer. This cooking method requires less oil, resulting in a lower fat content. It is also more nutritious, because all the nutrients are retained in the food. Steaming meat, fish and Dim Sum are very popular and you can find some other recipes for these in different sections.

## Serves 2

### Ingredient
200g pork spare ribs
100g mooli (oriental white turnip)

### Seasoning
2 tablespoons Yangjiang fermented
  black beans
2 cloves of garlic, peeled and crushed
  finely
1 medium hot red chilli deseeded
  and cut in rings
1 teaspoon light soy sauce
1 tablespoon vegetable cooking oil
½ teaspoon corn flour
1 spring onion finely chopped

## Method

- Use a meat cleaver to cut the spare ribs into 3cm pieces. Peel and cut the turnip into 12 X 3cm square pieces.

- Rinse the fermented black beans and use the back of a tablespoon to press the beans lightly without mashing them.

- Marinade the spare ribs with the crushed garlic, light soy sauce, oil and fermented black beans. Add the corn flour to the spare ribs and then add the red chillies.

- Using a wok or large steamer, boil 1/3 of water in the wok/pan. If using a wok, stand a steaming rack in the boiling water. Ensure the water level is not above the rack. If using a steamer, fill the required volume of water as recommended in the instruction booklet.

- Using a round dish, a size that will fit in the steamer, lay the turnip squares side by side in the dish to form a base, arrange the marinaded spare ribs on top of the turnip squares. Covered tightly with a lid and steam for 15 minutes. The heat and moisture of the steam should cook both turnips and the spare ribs

- Before serving, put the finely chopped spring onion on top and drizzle 1 tablespoon vegetable oil. This dish is best served with boiled rice.

# Dong Bor Braised Belly Pork

This is a dish named after the famous Song Dynasty Chinese poet Su Dong Bor. During his self-exiled years (1080-1090) in Hangzhou, in the South China province, he described the cooking process of this dish in one of his poems. People believed that apart from being a poet, scholar and politician, Su Dong Bor was also a culinary expert.

## Serves 4-5

### Ingredients
500g pork belly
2 tablespoons vegetable cooking oil

### Seasoning
2 pieces star anise
2 bay leaves
½ cinnamon stick
3 teaspoons dark soy sauce
4 teaspoons oyster sauce
3 teaspoons light soy sauce
1 teaspoon sugar
1 meat stock cube diluted in 1 litre water
1 tablespoon rice wine

### Thickening
1 teaspoon cornflour
3 tablespoons water

### Condiments
5 small pak choi

## Method

- Clean and dry the pork belly. Using a small sharp knife lightly score the pork belly into 9 (3cm X 3cm) equal pieces. Then, using a meat cleaver, cut according to the markings, keeping them together as one piece.

- Heat a wok or frying pan to moderate heat. Pour in 2 tablespoons vegetable oil. Carefully place the pork belly into the work, skin-side down first and fry for 2 minutes. Turn each piece belly pork skin-side up to fry for another 2 minutes.

- Put all the seasoning ingredients into the wok, cover with a lid and braised for 45 minutes.

- Wash the pak choi, drain off excess water. If using a wok, five minutes before finishing cooking, arrange the pak choi around the meat and cover with a lid. The heat from the cooking should be sufficiently hot enough to cook the pak choi inside the work.

- When you have finished cooking, remove the pak shoi and arrange around the edge of a serving dish. Remove all the seasoning spices. Use a spatula to carefully take out the cooked pork belly. This can be arranged on the serving dish skin-side up circled by pak choi.

- Discard any remaining seasoning spices. Mix the corn flour with 3 tablespoons water. Pour the liquid into the remaining sauce in the wok. Stir well until the sauce thickens. Pour the sauce on top of the pork belly. It is now ready to serve.

# Fillet Steak in Fruity Sauce

Discover this fruity favour of a Hong Kong style fillet steak. It is usually served on a sizzling hot plate in the restaurant. The tender texture of the fillet goes especially well with the slightly sweet and sour fruity sauce.

## Serves 2-3

### Ingredients

500g fillet of beef
1 medium onion
½ green pepper
½ red or yellow pepper
2 tablespoons vegetable cooking oil

### Sauce

4 teaspoons white rice vinegar
3 teaspoons tomato puree
5 teblespoons fresh orange juice
1 tablespoon sugar
⅓ teaspoon salt
1 teaspoon cornflour

## Method

- Cut the fillet of beef into 1cm thick slices. Marinade with 1 tablespoon vegetable cooking oil.

- Slice the onion and pepper into thin strips

- Heat a wok or frying pan to a high heat - until smoke rises when you pour oil in. Pour 2 tablespoons of vegetable cooking oil into the wok. Swirl the oil around the wok or frying pan. First stir-fry the beef on both sides for 2 minutes. Add the onion and peppers. Mix all the sauce ingredients and pour these into the wok. Blend the sauce well with the beef, onion and peppers until it thickens. Turn the heat down to moderate and continue to cook for a further 2 more minutes. Best served immediately with rice.

# Stewed Chu-Hou Beef Brisket

This dish is named after a Cantonese chef in Guangdong province during the Qing Dynasty; chef Chu-Hou. He owned a small diner which he prepared and served the local community. Used cheap cuts of meat such as beef brisket to prepare the dishes. He also concocted a sauce based on a fermented yellow-bean paste and other secret ingredients. He would add the sauce to beef which he stewed until it was very tender. Beef was very expensive at the time, even cheap cuts. He thought by adding turnips to the stew, he could get more portions out of the dish. It turned out to be a brilliant idea as the turnips absorbed all the favours from the stew. He decided to produce the sauce under his name, for people to use in their own cooking stew. The rest is history!

## Serves 4-5

### Ingredients
500g beef brisket or stewing beef
300g mooli (Chinese turnip)
2 tablespoons vegetable cooking oil

### Seasoning
4 tablespoon Chu-Hou sauce (available from most Chinese supermarket)
2 star anise
1 teaspoon oyster sauce
1 tablespoon light soy sauce
1½ teaspoon dark soy sauce
1½ teaspoon sugar
⅓ teaspoon sesame seeds oil
1 tablespoon cooking rice wine
20g ginger
⅓ teaspoon ground pepper
1 beef stock cube diluted in 1.5 litre water
1 medium hot green chilli (optional)
1 medium hot red chilli (optional)

### Thickening
1 tablespoon cornflour
3 tablespoons water

## Method

- Cut the beef brisket approximately 3cm X 4cm cubes. Peel the turnips and cut diagonally to a similar size as the beef. Deseed both chillies and cut them into rings. Cut the ginger in slices.

- Using a heavy based saucepan, pour 2 tablespoons of vegetable cooking oil into the pan. Heat the cooking oil up and then add the beef and glaze evenly, ensuring that the beef does not stick to the pan.

- Keep the turnips and chillies aside to use later. Add all the seasoning ingredients, including the diluted beef stock, into the pan. Stir a few times and cover with a lid to stew the beef on a moderate heat for approximately 50 minutes or until the meat texture became tender.

- Add all the turnip pieces in the pot, stir well, cover the lid to stew for another 20 minutes.

- Before serving, add the chillies and the corn flour to the liquid in the pot. Stir the stew while you are pouring the liquid in. Continue to stir for a further 2 minutes.

- Turn the heat off and let the stew stand for 20 minutes. Reheat before serving. Serve on a bed of lettuce (optional) in a serving bowl.

*Useful tips:* If preferred, reheat any left over meat and sauce, this makes a delicious meal when served with boiled noodle.

素菜

# Main Course - Vegetarian

# Fried Tofu in Hot and Sour Sauce

Fried tofu in hot and sour sauce is a popular Beijing snack, but it is equally delicious and appetizing as a main course. Crispy on the outside, with a soft texture inside. Deep-fried tofu is a winter warmer; whether drizzle over with sweet and sour sauce with a hint of hot chilli or dipped it, it makes it a special vegetarian dish. In  Beijing markets, the street vendors would favour the tofu with spices, skewer the tofu cubes with a bamboo stick and deep-fried; you can smell the aroma miles away.

## Serves 1-2

### Ingredient

500g firm tofu
½ onion
½ green and red peppers
1 ½ - 2 litres of vegetable cooking oil
   (for frying)

### Sauce

½ teaspoon chilli powder
½ tablespoon white rice vinegar
3 teaspoons sugar
4 teaspoons tomato puree(or ketchup)
2½ tablespoons water

### Condiments

Green part of the spring onion, finely
   chopped

## Method

- Using several layers of kitchen paper towel, drain the excess water from the tofu. Cut the tofu into 3cm square cubes, then cut green and red peppers to a similar size.

- In an electric deep-fryer, Heat the oil to 220°C or vegetable setting. When the oil is heated, put few tofu cubes into the fryer (frying only a few cubes at a time will prevent the tofu releasing water into the oil and lowering its temperature). Fry until golden brown (it will take only 5-6 minutes for the tofu to become firm and crisp), remove from fryer and drain off the excess oil on kitchen paper towel. When all the tofu has been fried, put all the pepper and onion cubes into the fryer to fry for 2 minutes, then drain off excess oil on some kitchen paper towels.

- In a saucepan, boil 2½ tablespoons of water, blend in all the sauce ingredients, stirred well then simmer for 2 minutes.

- Arrange the tofu and fried peppers and onion together in a serving dish, drizzle the sauce on top then sprinkle with chopped spring onion. Serve at once.

# Gai Lan in Ginger Sauce

Gai lan, also known as Chinese broccoli, is rather different to its western cousin. It is available in all Chinese supermarkets. Gai lan is one of the most versatile green vegetables eaten by the Chinese; it can be stir-fried, cooked in soup or boiled and drizzled with oyster sauce. However, frying in ginger sauce is the most common way of cooking gai lan, as the ginger brings out the sweet, pleasant taste of this vegetable.

## Serves 1-2

### Ingredient
350g Gai lan
20g fresh ginger

### Seasoning
2 tablespoons vegetable cooking oil
½ teaspoon salt
½ teaspoon sugar
1 tablespoon rice cooking wine (optional)

### Thickening
½ teaspoon corn flour
2 tablespoons water

## Method

- Wash the gai lan and cut them into half lengthways, or, if preferred, keep them in whole.

- Peel the fresh ginger, grated half and finely shred the other half.

- Boil a litre of water in the wok or a large saucepan. Blanch all the gai lan in the boiling water for one minute, then place in a colander and either plunge them into a bowl or cold water or run cold water over them. This technique will help soften the gai lan while still keeping them green when cooked. Drain off the excess water.

- Heat the wok or large saucepan to a very high heat, add 2 tablespoons of vegetable cooking oil, then pour both grated and shredded ginger into the wok and stir rapidly to prevent burning. Add the blanched gai lan to the wok immediately, stir for a minute and then add salt and sugar (and rice cooking wine) to blend in the gai lan, without covering the wok or lowering the heat, cook for a further one minute.

- Before serving, mix the corn flour with 2 tablespoons water, add the liquid to the wok and blend in until the sauce thickens. Served at one.

*Useful tip:* If preferred, you can add one tablespoonful of rice wine or brandy to the gai lan during cooking, do beware, alcohol can catch fire on the gai lan but evaporate very quickly.

# Lo-Hon Monks' Vegetables

Traditionally, this dish was only served in buddhist temples during festive celebrations. Combining 18 different dried and fresh vegetables, this vegetarian dish was named after the 18 Shaolin buddhist monks. For their followers, eating this vegetarian dish reminded them of the practice of 'good conduct', 'mental development' and 'wisdom', the buddhist teachings they strive to achieve. Over the years, the dish has grown more and more popular, and no longer the reserve of the followers of buddhism. The nutritional value of all the ingredients combined certainly helps toward achievement of the monk's teachings of good conducts, mental development and wisdom.

## Serves 2-4

## Ingredients

30g wood-ear dried fungus
20g dried day lily buds
10g dried cellophane noodles
20g dried bean curd sticks
30g tinned arrowhead mushrooms
30g tinned Chinese mushrooms or fresh
  button mushrooms
20g tinned bamboo shoot slices
20g tinned water chestnut, sliced
10g sliced carrot
30g mange-tout or sugar snaps
30g baby sweetcorns

## Seasoning

½ teaspoon salt
⅓ teaspoon sugar
1 tablespoon Oyster sauce
2 tablespoons vegetable cooking oil

## Thickening

1 teaspoon corn flour
3 tablespoons water

## Method

■ Rehydrate all the dried ingredients by soaking them in water separately for 30 minutes.

■ If using dried mushrooms, they require boiling in the water for 30-45 minutes with the dried bean curd sticks or until they are completely rehydrated. Remove the stems from mushrooms and cut the bean curd sticks into 3cm lengths.

■ Drain off the excess waters from all the rehydrated and tinned ingredients.

■ Heat the wok or frying pan to a high heat, so that smoke rises when you pour oil in. Swirl the oil around the wok, add all the ingredients to stir-fry for 5 minutes except the cellophane noodles. Then, add the cellophane noodles, salt, sugar and a little water, cover with the lid and without lowering the heat, cook for a further 3 minutes.

■ Before serving, add the diluted corn flour liquid to the wok and blend in until the sauce thickens. Serve at once.

*Useful tips:* All the ingredients used in this recipe are available in all Chinese supermarkets

# Chinese Mushrooms in Oyster Sauce

Mushrooms braised in oyster sauce is a traditional Cantonese dish. Adding oyster sauce when cooking vegetable is very typical in Cantonese cuisine, the sweetness of the sauce combining the earthy texture of the Chinese mushroom, makes this dish incredibly appetizing.

## Serves 1-2

### Ingredient
6 large Chinese mushroom

### Seasoning
2 tablespoons oyster sauce
⅔ teaspoon sugar
½ cup water

### Thickening
1 teaspoon corn flour
3 tablespoons water

### Condiments
½ iceberg lettuce (washed)

*Useful tip:* Fresh Shitaki mushrooms are not suitable to use in this recipe, the watery texture of Shitaki mushroom after cooking will leave you very little to eat. You can use reconstitute tinned mushroom instead, just drain the water and braised the mushrooms, but cut the cooking time to 3 minutes.

## Method
- Remove the stems from the mushrooms and score a cross on the top of each one to help absorption of the sauce during cooking.

- Rehydrate the mushrooms either by soaking them in water overnight, or boiling them in water for 30 minutes, then drain and squeezy out excess water.

- Heat the wok to a very high heat, add 2 tablespoons vegetable cooking oil then swirling the oil around to coat the wok surface. Put all the lettuce leaves in the wok and toss rapidly for 20 second, add a little salt to taste, then remove from heat and put in a bowl for later use.

- Clean and dry the wok, add 2 tablespoons of vegetable cooking oil into the wok , then add the mushrooms, water, oyster sauce and sugar to braise for 15 minutes on a moderate heat. Dilute the corn flour in the water, blend the liquid in the mushroom, cook until the sauce thickens. Turn off the heat.

- In a serving dish, make a layer of the slightly wilted lettuce leaves, make sure that any liquid has been removed from the lettuce first. Arrange the braised mushrooms on top, pour in the remaining sauce and serve at once.

# Pei Pa Tofu

Pei pa tofu is a traditional Cantonese vegetarian dish In this recipe, it is cooked and served in a Chinese soup spoon to resemble the classical Chinese musical instrument, the Pei Pa.

## Serves 2-3

### Ingredient
300g firm tofu
2 spring onions finely chopped
1 litre vegetable cooking oil

### Seasoning
½ teaspoon salt
⅓ teaspoon sugar
¼ teaspoon sesame seed oil
¼ teaspoon ground pepper
¼ teaspoon oyster sauce (optional)
2 tablespoons self-raising flour
2 tablespoons corn flour

## Method

- Drain any excess water from the tofu, put in a large bowl then use a tablespoon to slightly mash it.

- Add all the seasoning ingredients into the bowl and mix to a paste with the tofu.

- Using 6 Chinese soup spoons, dip one into a bowl of water to 'wet' it, then use it to scoop the paste into the soup spoons, fill the paste above the rim of the spoon and forms a smooth mount of tofu as illustrated. Use the same method to fill all the spoons

- set the temperature of an electric deep-fryer to 220°C, using the recommended minimum volume of oil. When the oil is heated, put the tofu spoons in the oil to fry one at a time for 5 minutes each.

- Remove the spoon from fryer when cooked (the tofu should look golden brown). Drain off the excess oil on kitchen paper towels, then use more paper towel to clean the oil from the handle of the spoon. Before serving, sprinkle a little chopped spring onion onto the tofu. Serves them on an oblong serving dish.

*Useful tips: Do not use plastic and melamine spoons for this recipe, only ceramic Chinese spoons are suitable for deep-frying with the tofu.*

# Fried Potato, Pepper & Aubergine

Three fresh vegetables combine to make this traditional northern Chinese dish. The softness of aubergine, the earthiness of the potato and the crunchiness of the pepper make it an unusual, yet very tasty, dish. It is also very easy and quick to make and is suitable for vegetarians.

## Serves 1-2

### Ingredients
1 aubergine
1 large potato
½ green pepper
½ red pepper

### Seasoning
2 tablespoons oyster sauce
2 teaspoons light soy sauce
1 teaspoon sugar

### Thickening
1 teaspoon corn flour
3 tablespoons water

## Method

- Peel the potato and cut into 3-4 cm small wedges. Cut the aubergine and green and red peppers to a similarly size.

- In an electric deep-fryer, heat the oil to the vegetable setting. When the oil is heated, deep-fry the potato wedges until golden brown, remove from fryer and drain off excess oil on kitchen paper towel.

- Next, fry the aubergine, this will only take 3-5 minutes. Before taking out the aubergine, put all the peppers into the fryer to fry for one minute. Remove all the vegetables from fryer and drain off excess oil.

- Heat a wok or frying pan to moderate heat then, without adding any oil, put all the fried vegetables into the wok and toss them around to reheat them. Add all the seasonings to the vegetables and cook for 5 minutes, stirring occasionally. Dilute the cornflour with 3 tablespoonful of water and pour the liquid into the vegetables. Cook until the sauce thickens.

- Serve the fried vegetables on a serving dish.

# Spicy and Sour Shredded Potatoes

The potato and Chinese cuisine may seem an unusual combination. However, few people realise that since the 1970s, China has been producing potatoes, and that, today, China is the world's largest potato producing country. Naturally, this tuberous crop has found its way into the local cuisine.

## Serves 3-4

## Ingredients

500g large waxy or all rounder potato
2 celery stalks cut in thin strips
1 spring onion finely chopped
2 cloves of garlic finely crushed
8-10 dried red chillies
1 tablespoon Szechuan peppercorns
3 tablespoon vegetable cooking oil

## Seasoning

½ teaspoon salt
2 tablespoons sugar
4 tablespoons white wine vinegar
½ teaspoon sesame seed oil

## Method

- Pour 6 cups of cold water into a large bowl and add 3 tablespoons of sea salt. Peel and wash the potatoes, sliced the potato to 5mm slices then, once you have cut 3-4 slices, stack them and cut them into thin strips. Soak the potato strips in the salt water. Carry on in the same way until all the potatoes have been cut.

- It is important to soak the potatoes in the salt water to prevent them turning brown. Once the potato shreds have been soaked for 15 minutes, rinse them under cold tap water to wash away the starch. Drain away the excess water then carefully pat the potatoes dry without breaking them.

- Mix all the seasoning ingredients together in a bowl, then leave aside to use later.

- Heat 3 tablespoons vegetable cooking oil in the wok over a moderate heat, swirl the oil around the wok evenly to prevent the potato sticking. Sauté the Szechuan peppercorns and dried chillies in the oil for 20 seconds, add the garlic and stir for 20 seconds, then add the celery and potato strips to the wok and toss and stir with the wok/frying spatula. Add the seasoning half way through cooking. Add the liquid to the potatoes and continue toss and stir-fry until the liquid in the wok has evaporated, taking care not to overcook the potatoes.

- Before serving, garnish with chopped spring onion.

*Useful tip:* It is not necessary to eat the chillies unless you are used to the heat, like the peppercorns, they are used for the aroma rather than the taste.

# Vegetarian Foo Yung Egg

Foo Yung egg is an omelette dish made with beaten egg, meat and vegetables. However, this vegetarian version is a more elaborate, using fresh and dried ingredients together, so that the different colours and the soft texture of the egg resemble the many layers of a lotus flower. With this recipe, plus a little creative flair, you can impress the most discerning eaters amongst your friends and family.

## Serves 2

### Ingredients
6 free range eggs
4-5 pieces dried wood-ear fungus
2 halves of tinned bamboo shoots
1 carrot
a quarter of green and red pepper each
A handful of bean sprouts

### Seasoning
½ teaspoon salt
¼ teaspoon ground white pepper
½ teaspoon sesame seed oil

### Garnish
few fresh chives

## Method

■ Soak the wood-ear fungus in boiling water, once rehydrated, discard the woody end of the fungus, wash and finely cut into thin strips.

■ Peel the carrot, cut diagonally into thin slices, then stack the slices together and cut into thin strips. cut the bamboo shoots and peppers in the same way. Remove the the brown ends from the bean sprouts, wash and drain off excess water before cooking.

■ Heat the wok or frying pan to a moderate heat, add 2 tablespoons of oil and heat until smoke rises. Add all the finely cut vegetable strips to the wok and stir-fry. Mix in all the seasonings and continue stir-fry until the liquid from the vegetables has completely evaporated. Remove from wok and keep aside.

■ Beaten all 6 eggs in a large bowl and put to one side.

■ Wash and dry the wok, then heat it to moderate heat, add 4 tablespoons of oil and swirl around the wok. Pour the beaten egg into the wok and fry it like an omelette, adding the cooked vegetables before the egg begins to set. Mix the vegetables with the egg and cook until the eggs have set.

■ Place a setting ring on the serving plate, fill the ring with Foo Yung egg until slightly overflowing, and then press slightly down to help the egg stick together. Remove the ring carefully then garnish the egg with 2 strips of fresh chives. Serve immediately.

饭·面
菜譜

# Rice and Noodles

# Egg Fried Rice

Rice is the staple food for all Asian. There are different rices used in Chinese cuisines, but long grain rice is the type of rice used in this book rice recipes. Although Chinese mainly eat boiled rice, but fried rice is more popular for non Chinese. Egg fried rice is the base of all other fried rice dishes featured in this book.

## Serves 2-3

### Ingredients

500g boiled rice
2 medium eggs (beaten)
15g frozen peas (defrosted)
1 tablespoon finely chopped spring
   onion
25ml vegetable cooking oil

### Seasoning

½ teaspoon salt
¼ teaspoon sesame seed oil
¼ teaspoon white ground pepper

## Method

- Pour oil into a very hot wok or frying pan, and swirl around to coat the surface.

- Pour the beaten egg into the wok and stir vigorously, add peas and stir into the egg.

- Loosen the rice with a pair of chopsticks before adding it to the wok, then mix well with the egg and peas. Stir in all the seasoning ingredients. Add the chopped spring onion, stir well and serve immediately.

## How to prepare boiled rice

- Although the Chinese use a rice cooker to prepare boiled rice. You can also cook rice in a medium size non-stick saucepan that come with a lid.

- Use 1 cup of rice, wash and rinse twice. Then, using an index finger as a guide of the correct level, add water to cover above the rice. With the tip of your index finger touching the surface of the rice, the water level should reach the first knuckle.

- Cook your rice over a moderate heat. When the water is boiling, turn the heat down and simmer until all the water has evaporated. There is no need to stir the rice during cooking. Do not drain off the water, as the rice needs to absorb all the water in order to puff up. Simmer the rice for 5 minutes over a very low heat with the lid covered tightly, turn off the heat and let the rice stands for another 5 minutes.

- Serves hot or use the rice for cooking fried rice.

# Yung Chow Fried Rice

An imperial rice dish served during the Qing dynasty, the recipe was introduced by an imperial chef named the rice dish after the region of Yangchou. It was introduced to UK in 1884 at International Health Exhibition.

## Serves 3-4

## Ingredients

500g boiled rice
2 medium eggs (beaten)
50g frozen shrimps (defrosted)
50g Cha Siu (roast pork) or cooked
  chicken
15g frozen peas (defrosted)
1 tablespoon finely chopped spring
  onion
25ml vegetable cooking oil

## Seasoning

½ teaspoon salt
¼ sesame seeds oil
¼ white ground pepper

## Method

■ Pour oil into a very hot wok or frying pan, and swirl around to coat the surface

■ Pour the beaten egg into the wok and stir vigorously, add peas and stir into the egg.

■ Before adding the rice to the wok, add the peas, shrimps and meat and stir-fry for 3 minutes.

■ Loosen the rice with a pair of chopsticks before adding it to the wok, then stir to mix well with the rest of the ingredients already cooked inside the wok. Add all the seasoning ingredients and mix well. Add the chopped spring onion, stir well and served immediately.

# Yin Yang Fried Rice

The philosophy of yin and yang lies at the heart of Chinese culture. Yin Yang Fried Rice is always served at the end of a wedding banquet, to symbolize the harmony between man and wife in their future.

## Serves 3-4

### Ingredients
400g boiled rice
1 medium egg, beaten
20ml vegetable cooking oil

### Seasoning
⅓ teaspoon salt
⅓ teaspoon Chicken powder

### Yin Sauce
4 king prawns, removed shell
20ml tin evaporated milk (unsweetened)
15g frozen peas, defrosted
⅓ teaspoon salt
250ml water
10ml vegetable cooking oil
1 tablespoon cornflour

### Yang Sauce
80g boneless chicken, cut in small strips
1 tomato, cut in 4 pieces
20g tomato puree
⅓ teaspoon salt
1 tablespoon White rice wine vinegar
3 teaspoons sugar
10ml vegetable cooking oil
250ml water
1 tablespoon cornflour

## Method
- Pour oil into a very hot wok or frying pan, and swirl around to coat the surface

- Pour the beaten egg into the wok and stir vigorously.

- Loosen the rice with a pair of chopsticks before adding it to the wok, then add seasonings, mix well and stir-fry for 3 minutes.

- put the plain fried-rice in a large round serving dish.

## To make Yin Sauce
- First fry the prawns and peas in a clean wok with oil or frying pan.  Use 250ml water to mix all the sauce ingredients including the evaporated milk, pour the mixture into the wok and bring it to the boil.  When the sauce has thickened, pour it into a bowl and keep warm to use later.

## To make Yang Sauce
- Fry the chicken and tomato pieces until they are just cooked.  Use 250ml water to mix all the sauce ingredients and bring to the boil.  When the sauce has thickened, pour the sauce over half of the fried rice.

- Pour the Yin sauce over the other half and the dish is now ready to serve.

*Useful tip:* Fried rice must be kept hot in a preheated oven while preparing the sauces

# Pineapple Fried Rice

Adding fresh fruit in rice is very common in southeast Asian countries. The addition of pineapple makes this dish visually appealing and simply mouth-watering.

## Serves 2-3

### Ingredients
1 large fresh pineapple
400g boiled rice
20g frozen peas (defrosted)
20g diced carrot
20g diced red and green peppers
1 medium egg (beaten)
40g fresh pineapple pieces

### Seasoning
½ teaspoon salt
30ml vegetable cooking oil

## Method

- Trimmed off the brown leaves and the spikes from the bottom of the pineapple. Cut the whole pineapple vertically into 2 halves.

- Carved out the pineapple flesh with a small shape knife. Discard the hard core from the pineapple and then cut the pineapple into small pieces, keep these aside to use later. Cover the hollow half of the pineapple with cling film while you are preparing the rice and other ingredients.

- Pour 30ml cooking oil into a very hot wok or frying pan, and swirl the oil around to coat the wok surface.

- Pour the beaten egg into the wok and stir vigorously, add peas, carrot, pineapple pieces, red and green peppers to stir well with the egg for 2 minutes.

- Loosen the rice with a pair of chopsticks before adding it to the wok, then stir to mix well with the rest of the ingredients already cooked inside the wok. Add salt and stir well.

- Serve the rice inside the hollow pineapple half. Garnishing the rice with coriander.

*Useful tip:* In addition, you can add prawns or chicken in the pineapple rice, fry it with the rest of the vegetables first before adding the rice.

# Chicken Fried Noodles

There are many different types of noodle used in Chinese cuisine. Noodle are a staple food for all Asians. The earliest written record of noodles is found in a book dated to the Eastern Han period (25-220 BC) of China. Most common noodles eaten by Asians are made from wheat flour, buckwheat flour, rice flour, mung bean flour, potato starch and cornmeal.

## Serves 1-2

## Ingredients

1 round of fine dried noodles
100g boneless chicken
15g carrot
50g bean sprouts
15g onion
10g spring onion
30ml vegetable cooking oil

## Seasoning

¼ teaspoon salt
½ teaspoon sugar
1 tablespoon light soy sauce

## Method

- Use a large saucepan to boil one litre of water. Put the dried noodles into the boiling water, and loosen the noodles with a pair of chopsticks or fork, until they are completely loosen, drain them in a colander and run cold water over the noodles for 30 seconds. Drain the excess water and put the noodles to one side.

- Wash the bean sprouts and drain off expense water. Cut the carrot in small, thin strips, cut the onion to a similar size, then cut the onion in 4-5 cm long pieces.

- Cut the chicken in 5cm strips, approximately 1cm thick.

- Heat a wok to very high heat, add oil and swirl around to coat the wok surface. Put the onion in the oil and fry before adding the chicken strips and fry for a further 3 minutes. Add the rest of the ingredients to the wok and stir well, then add the noodles to the wok and mix in with the meat and vegetables. Add all the seasoning, stir in, and fry for another 3 minutes.

- Garnish with coriander and serve at once.

*Useful tip:* Do not over-boiled the noodle, they will become soggy. Make sure the excess water completely drained and the noodles are very dry before stir-fry.

# Singapore-style Fried Noodles

The main ingredient of Singapore-style fried noodles is the thin noodles made from rice. It was served in Malaysian and Singapore restaurants originally, though this dish is now appears on the menu of almost all Chinese eateries worldwide.

## Serves 1-2

### Ingredients

150g dried rice noodle(vermicelli)
50g cooked shrimps
75g roasted pork (Cha siu) or chicken
15g carrot
15g green pepper
75g bean sprouts
2 spring onions
1 medium egg

### Seasoning

¼ teaspoon salt
1 teaspoon curry paste

## Method

- Defrost the shrimps if frozen, drain and dry with kitchen paper towel. Cut the roasted pork or chicken into thin strips

- Wash the bean sprouts and drain off excess water. Cut the carrot and green peppers in thin strips and the spring onion to 4-5 cm lengths. Beat the egg and leave to one side to use in the final stage of preparation.

- Boil a kettle of water, put the rice noodle in a mixing bowl and pour boiling water over them. Make sure the noodles are immersed in the boiling water, then cover the mixing bowl for 2 minutes or until they can be loosen, but not too soft.

- Drain the noodles in a colander and rinse under a cold water tap. Drain off the excess water, if possible leave them to dry .

- Heat a wok to a very high heat, pour in a little oil in and swirl around to coat the wok. Fry the beaten egg first in the wok, stirring it vigorously until it has an omelette-like consistency, remove the egg and put to one side. Pour the rest of the oil into the wok, add the pork/chicken and fry for about 3 minutes. Add the vegetables to the wok and stir well, then add the noodles and mix in with the meat and vegetables. Finally, add all the seasoning, mix, and fry for further 2 minutes. Before serving, add the fried egg to the noodles, mix well and serve immediately.

# Dan Dan Noodles

A classic Szechuan dish, the name "Dan Dan" refers to the way in which street vendor originally carried two baskets on each side of a pole on his shoulders, selling a soup noodle to passers-by and residents of the street.

## Serves 1-2

### Ingredients
100g white fresh wheat noodles
4 Chinese flowering cabbage
75g minced pork
20g green and red peppers
10g onion
100ml water

### Seasoning
¼ teaspoon salt
1 teaspoon chilli sauce
1 tablespoon rice vinegar
1 tablespoon light soy sauce

### Thickening
½ teaspoon cornflour
2 tablespoons water

### Garnish
½ medium hot red chilli
1½ tablespoon chopped spring onion

- In a large saucepan, boil 1.5 litre of water, when the water is boilling, add the noodles and the flowering cabbage into the saucepan and boil for 2 minutes. Drain and keep warm.

- Dice the onion, green and red peppers, put to one side. Deseed the red chilli and cut into rings. Finely chop the spring onion and keep for garnish.

- Heat a wok to very high heat, pour oil in and swirl around to coat the wok. Fry the onion first, then add the minced pork and fry for about a minute. Add the diced green and red peppers to the wok and stir-fry for 2 minutes.

- Add all the seasoning ingredients to the wok and 100ml water and simmer. Mix the corn flour with 2 tablespoons of water, pour the liquid into the wok and cook for 2 minutes.

- Arrange the boiled noodle and flowering cabbage in a serving dish. Pour the meat and sauce over the noodles, garnish with chilli and spring onion and serve immediately.

# Northeast China Cold Noodle Soup

The northeast region of China was historically know as Manchuria. Many dishes originated from Manchu cuisine, which combines fresh and preserved ingredients, Northeast cuisine is a new rising star among Chinese cuisines, cold noodle soup is one of its many specialities.

## Serves 1-2

### Ingredients
1 round of fine wheat noodle
100g fillet of beef
30g carrot
30g cucumber
1 tomato
1 fresh egg
1 duck egg
300ml water

### Seasoning
¼ teaspoon salt
½ teaspoon sugar
½ teaspoon chilli oil (optional)
2 tablespoon white rice vinegar
¼ teaspoon sesame seed oil
¼ teaspoon white ground pepper

## Method

■ Clean and boil the duck egg. Once cooled, remove shell and cut in 2 halves

■ Peel carrot and cucumber, cut both in thin strips, cut tomato in thin slices, keep them aside to use later.

■ Prepare the soup base by boiling 300ml water in a saucepan. Add all the seasoning ingredients to the water and simmer for one minute. Remove from heat and keep to one side.

■ Boil 500ml water in a clean saucepan, put the noodles in and boil for 2 minutes, loosening the noodles with a pair of chopsticks or folk. When soft, drain the noodle in a colander and rinse the noodles with cold water under the tap. Drain off excess water and keep to one side.

■ Heat a wok to very high heat, pour 2 tablespoons vegetable cooking oil into the wok and swirl around to coat the wok surface. Pour the beaten egg into the wok and swirl the egg around the wok to make until a thin, pancake-like layer forms. Remove the egg from wok and let it cool before cutting it into thin strips.

■ Using the same wok over a high heat, add one tablespoon of oil then, when the smoke rises from oil, add the fillet of beef and fry for one minute on each side. Turn off the heat and start to assemble the dish.

■ Place the cold noodle in a large soup bowl, pour soup over the noodles, arrange the vegetables, meat, fried egg and half of the boiled duck egg on top as illustrated. Serve at once.

# Won Ton Noodle Soup

Each region of China has its own variations of won ton, but none as famous as the Cantonese won ton soup with noodles. The secret of a good won ton noodle soup is the broth which, traditionally, is a clear soup made with pork bone and dried flounder (small flat fish). The won ton soup base is now widely available  from Chinese supermarket either in powder form in sachet or in small tin.

## Serves 1

### Main Ingredient
200g fresh noodle (1 round)
4 pieces fresh won ton skins
4 whole small bak choy
½ teaspoon finely chopped spring onion

### To make Won Ton
4 pieces fresh won ton skins
100g minced pork
½ teaspoon chicken powder
a pinch of salt
2 drops of sesame seed oil
a dash of white ground pepper

### To make from ready-made soup powder
1 heap teaspoon/1 sachet won ton soup
  powder if use ready-made soup base

### To make your own soup
1 pork leg bone
2 dried flounder
2 litres of water

## Method

- If you are making your own soup, prepare the soup 2 hours before cooking the noodles. Extra soup can be stored in freezer to use in the future.

- Mix the minced pork with the listed ingredients.  Place one sheet of wonton skin on a large plate, scoop one teaspoonful of the mixed raw meat onto the center of the wonton skin, then fold the 4 corners in and squeeze them together to make a little parce; the moisture from the meat should help the edges of the skin stick to one another.

- Boil 500ml of water in a clean saucepan, add the fresh noodles and boil for 2 minutes, loosening the noodles with a pair of chopsticks or folk. When the noodles are completely loosened, drain them in a colander then rinse the noodles with cold water under a tap. Drain off excess water and keep aside.

- Boil 200ml water in a saucepan, then add one teaspoon of wonton soup powder to make up the soup base. If you are using your own soup, simply use a clean saucepan to heat the 200ml soup to boiling point.  Wash the bak choy and put them in the soup with the wonton for 4 minutes, then add the pre-cooked noodles to the soup for another minute. Turn off heat and serve the noodle soup in a large soup bowl, garnished with chopped spring onion.

*Useful tip:* It is essetial to rinse the noodles with cold water, this process will prevent the noodles becoming soggy after boiling.

# Grilled Steak Ramen in Soup

Although the name "Ramen" is Japanese, but its of chinese origin, meaning "hand-pull noodles", the original way of making noodles. The Noodles are made from unleavened dough, the stretch and pull actions during the noodle making process enabling the dough to become separated strands of different thicknesses and shapes.

## Serves 2-3

## Ingredients

300g fresh ramen
180g fillet steak
20g wood ear fungus
30g cucumber
30g bean sprout
20g carrot
30g fresh golden needle mushroom
500ml water

## Seasoning

½ teaspoon salt
½ teaspoon chicken powder
⅕ teaspoon white ground pepper
⅕ teaspoon sesame seed oil

## Method

- Soak the wood ear fungi in boiling water. When they are rehydrated, discard the hard wooden part, cut in thin strips and put aside.

- Slice the fillet steak into 4 pieces and keep aside to cook later.

- Slices the carrot and cucumber, then cut them into thin strips, keeping each separately. There is no need to wash the golden needle mushroom.

- Boil 500ml water in a clean saucepan, put the fresh noodle in and boil for one minute. Use a wire strainer to scoop out the noodles and put into a noodle soup serving bowl. Next, add all the seasoning ingredients into the water to make soup. Boil the bean sprouts, carrot, wood-ear fungus and golden needle mushrooms individually for 2 minutes each. Carefully arrange each cooked vegetable on the noodles as illustrated.

- Heat a wok or frying pan over a very high heat, pour in 2 tablespoons vegetable cooking oil and swirl around to coat the wok. When oil starts to smoke, place the cut fillet steak into the wok and fry 30 seconds on each side (or longer if preferred).

- Top the noodle with cooked fillet steak and raw cucumber, serve at once.

# Seafood Udon Noodle Soup

Udon is a thick Japanese noodle served in hot soup. This noodle also made from wheat flour, though instead of pulling, the dough is usually rolled and stretched into a big flat sheet of the desired thickness, then cut into strands for cooking in a broth made with meat, seafood, or vegetables. Udon can also be made for stir-frying with the same ingredients. The udon noodles sold in supermarkets are usually precooked.

## Serves 4-5

### Ingredients

400g pack fresh udon
75g fresh king prawns
75g scallops
75g fresh squid
30g manger tout
30g carrot
30g fresh shitaki mushroom
500ml water

### Seasoning

1 tablespoon vegetable cooking oil
½ teaspoon salt
½ teaspoon chicken powder
¼ teaspoon sesame seed oil
¼ teaspoon ground white pepper
1 tablespoon Chinese cooking wine

## Method

- Remove the shells from prawns, score the back of each prawn half way through and remove vein.

- Clean and cut the squid into small squares, score the surface of one side horizontally, and then score vertically. If using frozen scallops, defrost first. Keep all the seafood together ready for cooking later.

- Cut the mushrooms into halves. Cut the carrots into thin strips. Wash and clean the mange tout; they can be cooked whole or cut diagonally into halves.

- Heat the wok to moderate heat and add oil. When the wok is hot enough, add all the seafood and stir-fry for one minute.

- Without removing the seafood from the wok, turn up the heat, add 500ml water and bring to boil. Add all the seasoning ingredients to the water, then add all the vegetables and udon and continue cooking for 4 minutes.

- Turn off heat and serve udon in a large serving bowl.

# Dim Sum

# Steamed Beef Siu Mai

Siu Mai is a standard Chinese dim sum dish made with minced beef or pork, this is one of the hundreds of steamed dumpling dishes in Chinese cuisine. Some restaurants steamed beef siu mai on a little dish without the wonton skin, though in this recipe, the moisture of the minced beef sealed within the wonton skin has much better flavour.

## Makes 6

### Ingredients

200g minced beef
6 large wonton skins
5g dried tangerine skin
1 medium egg
15g water chestnut
6 peas

### Seasoning

⅓ teaspoon salt
⅓ teaspoon sugar
⅓ teaspoon light soy
½ teaspoon cornflour
¼ teaspoon sesame seed oil
¼ teaspoon white ground pepper

### Conditment

Worcester sauce or light soy sauce

## Method

- Rehydrate the dried tangerine skin in a small bowl of cold water for 2-3 hours. Finely chop the water chestnuts and the rehydrated tangerine skin.

- Place the minced beef on a large chopping board. Use the 'BLUNTED-EDGE' of the Chinese meat cleaver to beat the minced beef for 30 minutes, or, until the meat becoming a thick paste. This process will make the meat less chewy and avoid releasing meat juice during steaming. Then add the chopped water chestnut and tangerine skin to mix together, then add all the seasoning ingredients to blend in and mix well.

- Put an equal amount of the minced beef filling in the middle of each wonton skin until all the filling is used up.

- Snip off all 4 corners of the wonton skin. Fold the skin around the meat and shape into a little cup about 4cm tall as illustrated. Add a pea in the middle of each siu mai.

- Boil 200ml water in the wok, place a metal steaming rack in the middle of the wok, make sure the water level is well below the steaming rack. When the water is boiling, place the siu mai inside a bamboo steamer that comes with a lid, cover the lid and put the basket on the steaming rack that sits in the middle of the wok, cover the wok to steam in high heat for 20 minutes.

- Remove the basket and serve the siu mai on a plate.

# Cuttlefish Cake

Throughout Southeast Asia, cuttlefishes are plentiful and there are cuttlefish dishes such as dried, grilled, fried or braised in every Southeast Asian country, However, none as popular as cuttlefish cake. Cuttlefish can be very chewy on its own, but because it is minced and mixed with other ingredients in this recipe, the cakes have an irresistible fragrance and a very tender texture.

## Serves 1-2

### Ingredients
200g fresh cuttlefish (without tentacles)
1 medium rehydrated Chinese
   mushroom
1 tablespoon oil

### Seasoning
⅓ teaspoon salt
⅓ teaspoon sugar
⅓ teaspoon light soy
1 teaspoon cornflour
1 teaspoon finely chopped spring onion
¼ teaspoon sesame seed oil
¼ teaspoon white ground pepper

### Condiment
Dipping fish sauce:
*1 teaspoon fish sauce*
*1 tablespoon of water*
*2 teaspoons of vinegar*
*1 tablespoon of sugar*
*¼ teaspoon chopped fresh chilli*

## Method

- Clean the cuttlefish and remove the skin and all organs in its cavity. Cut the cuttlefish in small pieces.

- Use the blunted-edge of the meat cleaver to mince the cuttlefish, or use a food processor to mince the cuttlefish into a sticky paste.

- Put the minced cuttlefish into a bowl and add the chopped Chinese mushroom, mix together, then add all the seasoning ingredients and mix well.

- Use 2 serving spoons to shape the mixture into 3-4 little round cakes

- Heat a wok to very high heat, pour a tablespoon oil into the wok and swirl around to coat the wok, put the fish cakes into the wok, fry both sides for 5-7 minutes, or until golden brown. Served with salad.

*Useful tip: Instead of making dipping fish sauce, if preferred, use sweet chilli sauce as condiment.*

# Peach-Shaped Buns

Peach bun is one of the desserts served at banquet when people celebrate the birthdays for their elderly parents. The tradition can be traced back to the Chinese Warring States period. Around 316BC, China's most powerful military strategy writer, Szuanji, left home at 18 to learn military strategies. After 12 years away from home, he felt that he should go home to visit his elderly mother on her 80th birthday. Before he left, his master gave him a fresh peach to take home as a present for his mother. Legend has it that his mother became much younger after eating the birthday peach. Since then, it has been customary for Chinese people to bring peaches to their parents on their birthday as wishes for longevity. The peach shaped buns were made when fresh peaches were not in season.

## Makes 12 buns

### Ingredients for making dough

500g plain flour
100g sugar
300ml warm water
50ml vegetable cooking oil
5g dried yeast
5g baking powder
⅓ teaspoon red food colouring

### Filling

250g Lotus seed paste (ready made from tin)

### Green leaves (optional)

⅓ teaspoon green food colouring
*mix the green colouring with a little water, mix well into the dough, cut the dough in leaf-shape and score the surface, put the leaves on the dough ball as illustrated, then steam as directed.*

## To make the dough

- Measuring 300ml warm water in a jug, add sugar to dissolve. Put 500g flour in a large mixing bowl, add dried yeast and baking powder in the flour, then add the sugary water and oil to the flour to mix until a well-developed dough is formed, rest the dough for 10 minutes.

## Method

- Divide the dough into 12 pieces, roll each piece into a ball. Using a palm or a rolling pin, flatten the dough, then add 1 teaspoon (20g) of the filling to the middle of the dough, wrap the dough around the filling to form a ball.

- Use the back of a knife to press gently down the dough to create a groove. Mixed the red food colouring with a 3 tablespoons water in a small spray bottle, lightly spray onto the peach-shape dough ball.

- Keep the dough in a warm place for 1 hour, when ready, before steaming, add the leaf-shape dough onto the peach-shape dough, then place the dough into a bamboo basket, cover the basket with lid. Place the bamboo basket into a steamer to steam in high heat for 10 minutes. The buns are then ready to serve.

*Useful tip:* *When steaming the buns, give each bun a lot of room in the steamer, the buns expand to almost double the size. Uncooked buns can be frozen for up to 4 weeks, defrost before steaming.*

# Roast Pork Buns

Also called Cha Siu Bao, no Dim sum is completed without this Cantonese classic. The dough of the bun is used in many other steamed buns in Chinese cuisine. The customary filling is roast pork (Cha Siu).

## Makes 6 buns

## Ingredients for making dough

200g plain flour
10g sugar
120ml warm milk
5g dried yeast
5g baking powder
1½ teaspoon olive oil

## Filling

80g roast pork (cha siu)
1 teaspoon sugar
1 teaspoon dark soy sauce
1 teaspoon corn flour
2 teaspoons water chestnut flour
½ tablespoon vegetable cooking oil
200ml water
⅓ teaspoon red food colouring

## To make the filling

■ Cut the roast pork into 5mm cubes. Mixed soy sauce, corn flour, water chestnut flour and sugar with 100ml water. Preheat the wok over a moderate heat to fry the roast pork, add the flour liquid mixture into the wok and stir vigorously for 3 minutes. Leave the filling completely cool before use.

## To make the dough and buns

■ Measure 120ml warm milk in a jug, add sugar, dried yeast, stir well and leave the liquid to develop for 5 minutes.

■ Measure 200g plain flour in a large mixing bowl, add baking powder and the yeast liquid into the flour, mix until a well-developed dough is formed. Rest the dough for 5 minutes. With the palm of a hand rub ½ teaspoon olive oil over the surface of the dough. Cover the dough with a damp cloth and keep the dough in a warm place for 30 minutes or until doubles in size.

■ When the dough is ready, roll the dough to form a long tube and divide it into 6 equal pieces. Using both thumbs and index fingers squeeze the edges of the dough outwards until the dough is approximately 7cm diameter.

■ Put one tablespoon of filling in the middle of each piece of dough and wrap the dough around to form a little parcel. Twist the top of the dough to seal.

■ Place the dough into a bamboo basket and cover the basket with a lid. Place the bamboo basket into a steamer to steam on a high heat for 9 minutes. The buns are then ready to serve.

# Shanghai Style Dumplings

Shanghai style dumpling are also called Xiaolongbao, the name refers to buns steamed in a small bamboo basket. The classic Shanghai dumplings are made with unleavened hot dough and raw meat fillin. When steamed, the meat is cooked inside the dumpling and the juice from the meat sealed within. The result, when you bite into the dumpling, is an "eating dumpling in soup" experience.

## Makes 12

### Ingredients for making dough
350g plain flour
150ml boiling water

### Ingredients for filling
250g minced pork
½ teaspoon salt
½ teaspoon Chinese cooking wine
1 teaspoon grated ginger
2 teaspoons light soy sauce
4 tablespoons water
¼ teaspoon sesame seed oil
¼ teaspoon white ground pepper

### Sauce
2 tablespoons light rice vinegar
½ tablespoon finely shredded ginger

### Garnish
3 teaspoons salmon roe (optional)

## Method

- Prepare the filling first by mixing all the filling ingredients together. Roll the mixture into small meat balls no bigger than a 20 pence piece.

- Put flour into a mixing bowl, slowly pour boiling water into the flour and use a tablespoon to mix the flour to a soft dough. On a flour-covered surface, having dusted both hands with flour to avoid the dough sticking. Knead until a well-developed dough is formed. Roll the dough into a long tube.

- Divide the dough into 12 small pieces, roll each piece of dough into a ball, then use a rolling pin to flatten each dough ball until about 2mm thick and 7cm in diameter.

- Place a ball of raw meat filling onto the middle of each piece of dough, pleat the edges of the dough 5mm at a time and gradually close the dumpling. Squeeze the top and twist slightly to form a knob. Flatten the knob with a thumb and index finger to form a hollow space that can be filled the hollow space with a little salmon roe if desired.

- Lay a piece of lettuce leave inside the bamboo basket before placing the dumplings on top for steaming. If using a small bamboo basket, keep the dumplings apart from each other, leaving enough room for the dumplings to expand during steaming.

- Serves the dumplings with ginger vinegar.

# Steamed Pork Siu Mai

This is a luxurious version of steamed siu mai made with minced pork and a salmon roe topping. It is often served at fine-dining restaurants as a dim sum starter.

## Makes 6

## Ingredients

200g minced pork
6 large wonton skins
5g rehydrated tangerine skin
15g water chestnut
5g salmon roe

## Seasoning

⅓ teaspoon salt
⅓ teaspoon sugar
⅓ teaspoon light soy
⅓ teaspoon corn flour
¼ teaspoon sesame seed oil
¼ teaspoon white ground pepper

## Method

- Rehydrate the dried tangerine skin in a small bowl of cold water for 15 minutes. Finely chopped the water chestnuts and the rehydrated tangerine skin.

- Place the minced pork on a large chopping board. Use the 'BLUNTED-EDGE' of the Chinese meat cleaver to beat the minced pork for 30 minutes, or, until the meat becoming a thick paste. This process will make the meat less chewy and avoid releasing meat juice during steaming. Then add the chopped water chestnut and tangerine skin to mix together, then add all the seasoning ingredients to blend in and mix well.

- Snip off the 4 corners of the wonton skin. Place an equal amount of the minced pork filling in the middle of each wonton skin until all the filling is used up.

- Fold the skin around the meat and shape into a little cup about 4cm tall, as illustrated.

- Use a steamer or wok to boil 200ml water. Put a low steam rack in the water. Place the siu mai in a bamboo steaming basket that comes with a lid, put the basket into the wok when the water is boiling, cover the wok and steam on a high heat for 20 minutes.

- Remove the siu mai from basket and put on a plate, then add a ¼ teaspoonful of salmon roe on top of each siu mai. Serve at once.

# Boiled Peking Dumplings

Traditional Jiaozi is made with unleavened cold dough, similar to making ravioli except without egg in the dough. The dumpling filling typically consists of minced meat or vegetable. Peking dumplings can be steamed, boiled in soup, pan-fried or deep-fried. In China, Peking dumplings are eaten all year round and can be eaten at breakfast, lunch or dinner. This recipe is suitable for vegetarians.

### Serves 3-4

### Ingredients for making dough

400g dumpling flour (available in all Chinese supermarkets)
180ml water

### Ingredients for making filling

20ml vegetable cooking oil
300g thinly cut cabbage (Sweetheart)
100g thinly cut wood ear mushroom
1 teaspoon salt
1 teaspoon sugar
¼ teaspoon sesame seed oil
¼ teaspoon white ground pepper
1 teaspoon cornflour
1 tablespoon water

### Sauce for dipping

2 tablespoons light rice vinegar
2 tablespoons light soy sauce
1 tablespoon finely chopped spring onion
1 tablespoon finely chopped medium hot red chilli (optional)
½ teaspoon sesame seed oil

*Useful tip:* Raw dumplings can be frozen for up to 4 weeks, freeze the dumplings in a tray without stacking them together. Defrost before cooking.

### To make the filling

■ Rehydrate the wood ear mushroom in boiling water, removing the hard ends. When soft, thinly cut and put to one side. Wash the sweetheart cabbage leaves, remove the hard stalks from the leaves then cut thinly.

■ Preheat a wok to very high heat, pour oil and swirl around to coat the wok, then put the cabbage and wood ear mushroom in wok to stir-fry, add salt, sugar and white ground pepper to mix well, cover with lid and cook for 2 minutes or until soft. Mix one teaspoon of cornflour with one tablespoon of water, pour the liquid into the wok and blend in with the cabbage. Drain the cabbage in a colander and leave to cool.

### To make the dough

■ Put 400g dumpling flour in a large mixing bowl, add 180ml water to the flour and mix to a soft dough.

■ On a flour-covered surface, knead until a well-developed dough is formed. Roll the dough into a long tube then divide it into 35g pieces. Use a rolling pin to flatten each dough ball until about 2mm thick and 5cm in diameter.

### To make the dumpling

■ Put one tablespoon of cabbage filling onto the middle of each dough piece, fold the dough over, then seal the dough by pressing the edges together.

■ boiled the dumpling for 10 minutes. Cooked until all the dumplings are floating on the boiling water, spoon them out and served with dipping sauce.

# Steamed Prawn Dumplings

Prawn dumpling is called Ha Gow in Cantonese. It is a classic Cantonese dim sum, wrapped in the shape of a little bonnet. This dumpling is made with an unleavened mixture of wheat starch and cornflour. When cooked, the dumplings are slightly translucent, showing the colour of the cooked prawn inside. The pretty looks and delicious taste make these dim sum a must have dish for the Chinese.

## Serves 2-3

### Ingredients for making dough

200g wheat starch (available in all Chinese supermarkets)
50g corn flour
2/3 teaspoon salt
150ml boiling water
10ml vegetable cooking oil

### Ingredients for making filling

120g Bamboo shoot
125g fresh prawns
50g pork fat
10ml vegetable cooking oil
1/3 teaspoon sugar
1/3 teaspoon sesame seed oil
1/3 teaspoon white ground pepper

## To make the filling

- Cut the bamboo shoot into 2x3mm small pieces and soak in cold water. Pour little boiling water into a bowl, put the pork fat in the bowl for 30 seconds, then cut the pork fat into 3x3mm pieces.

- Remove the shells from prawns, clean and devein them, then press the prawns slightly. Drain off the excess water from the bamboo shoots and blot them dry with paper towel. Add the prawns and pork fat to the bamboo shoots, then add white ground pepper and sesame seed oil and mix by hand, squeezing the filling to form a ball. Put the filling into the freezer so that it hardens slightly while preparing the dough.

## To make the dough

- Put 200g wheat starch, 50g corn flour and salt in a large mixing bowl, slowly pour 150ml boiling water and 10ml vegetable oil into the flour and mix to a soft dough.

- On a flour-covered surface, knead the dough until a well-developed dough is formed. Roll the dough into a long tube, divide the dough into 25g pieces, use a rolling pin to flatten each of the dough pieces.

## To make the dumpling

- Remove the filling from the freezer and put one teaspoon of filling onto the middle of each piece of dough. Fold the dough over, then pleat 2/3 of the dough edges before pressing the remaining edges together to form a bonnet shape. Finish wrapping all the dough in this way.

- Steam the dumpling for 7 minutes then serve at once.

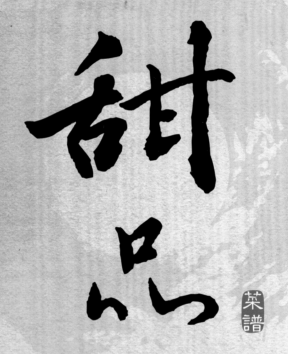

甜品

# Desserts

# Banana Fritter

Frying fruits in batter and eating with sugary syrup are very popular in northeast China. Traditionally, Bananas were grown in the warmer climate in the south-east Asia countries, the fruits are much smaller with very thin skin. Because they are very rare in the northeast of China, the fruit was one of the many delicacies for imperial consumption, hence the name "Kung Chiu" meaning divine banana.

## Serves 1-2

### Ingredients

2 banana
30ml golden syrup
1½ litre of vegetable cooking oil

### For the batter

120g self-raising flour
½ teaspoon baking powder
150ml cold water

## Method

- Put the self-raising flour into a mixing bowl, sprinkle the baking powder on top and add 150ml cold water to mix the batter, when the batter smooth, leave it to ferment for 30 minutes before use.

- Preheat the deep-fryer to 200°C with 1½ litre of vegetable cooking oil.

- Cut each banana into 3 or 4 pieces. Dip all the banana pieces into the batter and coat completely, then carefully put the batter-coated banana into the fryer and fry until golden yellow.

- Remove the fritters and place on kitchen paper towel to drain off excess oil.

- Serve the banana fritters on a serving dish and drizzle golden syrup over before serving.

# Toffee Apple

Like banana, apple is another fruit that can be fried in batter to make a delicious dessert.

## Serves 2

### Ingredients

1 large apple (preferably Golden Delicious)
300g granulated sugar
1 tablespoon golden syrup
40ml water
1 teaspoon white sesame seeds
2 litres of vegetable cooking oil

### For the batter

120g self-raising flour
150ml cold water

## Method

- Prepare the batter ahead of cooking. Mix 150g self-raising flour in 120ml of cold water, mix well until all the lumps have disappeared.

- Preheat an electric deep-fryer to high setting (200°C) with 2 litre of oil, or the manufacturer's recommended maximum volume.

- Peel off the apple skin, remove the core and cut the apple into 3cm X 3cm cubes. When the oil has reached the required temperature, dip all the apple cubes into the batter, making sure the batter has coated each piece completely.

- Put each piece of batter-covered apple into the deep-fryer separately and fry until golden yellow, turning the apple to ensure an even result.

- Drain off excess oil from the fried apple pieces on kitchen paper towel.

- Prepare the syrup with 40ml of water and 20ml of oil in a preheated wok, add 300g sugar and 1 tablespoon of golden syrup and boil until the syrup thickens. Turn the heat off and put all the fried apple pieces into the syrup and rapidly toss the apple to let the syrup form a semi sticky coat, sprinkle the white sesame seeds and serve immediately on a serving dish.

*Useful tip:* *For crunchy toffee coating, use 400g sugar and 40ml water to make syrup, after coating the fried apple pieces completely with the syrup, and then sprinkled sesame seeds, dip the toffee apple pieces into a bowl of coat water and remove immediately, the cold water hardens the syrup to a crunchy toffee coating.*

# Coffee Jelly

Coffee Jelly is a new way of combining dessert with after dinner coffee, all in one; it is easy to make and delicious to eat.

## Serves 3-4

### Ingredients

3 tablespoons gelatine powder
3 tablespoons sugar
2 teaspoons instant coffee granules
3 tablespoons condensed milk
200ml hot water

## Method

- Using a jug to dissolve 3 tablespoons of gelatine powder in 200ml hot water, when the gelatine has dissolved, add coffee granules and sugar and stir well until completely dissolved.

- Line a small square baking tray with a sheet of cling film and pour the gelatine liquid into the tray. Leave the tray in a refrigerator or cooler to set - this will take about an hour.

- When the jelly is set, remove from tray and cut it into bite size cubes.

- Serve the jelly in a pudding glass and drizzle condensed milk over before serving.

# Colourful Jelly

Gelatine dessert has come a long way since its day as a treat for children. Nowadays, adding different fruit flavours to make a colourful jelly is very popular in restaurants, and it is refreshingly delicious and delightful way to end a meal.

## Ingredients

**Yellow layer**
4 tablespoons lime jelly powder
4 tablespoons sugar
200ml hot water

**White layer**
4 tablespoons gelatine powder
4 tablespoons sugar
200ml hot milk

**Orange layer**
4 tablespoons orange jelly powder
4 tablespoons sugar
200ml hot water

**Chocolate layer**
4 tablespoons gelatine powder
4 tablespoons sugar
3 tablespoon chocolate powder
160ml hot milk

**Red layer**
4 tablespoons strawberry jelly powder
4 tablespoons sugar
200ml hot water

## Method

- Using a jug to dissolve the strawberry fruit jelly powder with 200ml hot water. When the powder has dissolved, add sugar and stir well until completely dissolved.

- Line a medium height square baking tray with a sheet of cling film, covering the tray bottom and sides completely and ensuring all 4 corners are well tucked in. Pour the strawberry jelly liquid into the tray, then place the tray in a refrigerator or cooler for about an hour while the jelly sets.

- To prepare the chocolate layer, warm 160ml milk in a saucepan to just below boiling point and stir in the sugar and chocolate powder. Pour the chocolate milk into a jug, add the plain gelatine powder and stir well until completely dissolved.

- Make sure the strawberry jelly layer is completely set then pour the chocolate jelly on top. Return the tray to the refrigerator or cooler to set, which should take another hour.

- Prepare the orange, white and yellow layers the same way. Make sure the previous layer is completely set before adding each new layer on top.

- When all five layers are set, remove from the tray and discard the cling film. Cut into 3cm X 4cm pieces, serve on a large plate or small individual plates as required.

*Useful tip:* If you have a freezer is big enough to hold the tray, use it to speed up the setting process.

# Green Tea and Red Bean Cake

An innovative way to combine dessert with tea, green tea and red bean cake is one of the most popular desserts served in Hong Kong's fine-dining restaurants.

## Serves 8

### Ingredients for top filling

600ml double cream
1 teaspoon icing sugar
30g green tea powder

### Ingredients for cake

6 egg, separated egg yolk and white
200g caster sugar
100ml olive oil
200g plain flour
5g cream of tatar
1g baking powder

### Ingredients for red bean cream filling

100g dried red bean or ready cooked red bean from tin
300ml double cream
1 tablespoon icing sugar

## Method

- CAKE - Sift the flour and baking powder in a mixing bowl. In an electric mixer bowl, put 6 egg whites, cream of tartar, and 200g caster sugar and mix until it is stiff and can hold soft peaks. Next, whisk 6 egg yolks, blend in the flour first and then blend the egg white in with a scooping action until the mixture has a batter texture. Preheat the oven to 190°C. Line an 8 inch round baking tin, pour in the cake mixture and bake in the oven for 40 minutes or until golden brown.

- RED BEAN CREAM FILLING - Cook the red beans in water for 2 hours or until soft. When the beans are cooked, drain off the excess water and leave to cool and dry. Use an electric hand mixer or a standing mixer fitted with a whisk attachment, start to beat the double cream and icing sugar slowly. When the cream starts to thicken, increase the speed until the cream forms a soft peak. Mix the cooked beans into the cream with a scooping action.

- TOP FILLING - Whisk the double cream, sugar and icing sugar together, whisk until thicken that forms a soft peak.

- When the cake is completely cool, cut into 3 thin layers. Put the first layer of cake onto a cake base, spread the red bean cream filling to cover the layer completely, add another cake layer, then spread the layer with the same filling to cover the cake completely. Place the third layer of cake on top. Spread the top filling over the top layer of cake, smooth the surface, then sprinkle a thin layer of green tea powder to cover the cream.

- Divide the cake in 8 portions. Decorate the cake with fresh cream, strawberries and raspberries as illustrated. Chill the cake in a cake box until time to serve.

# Mango Pudding

Instead of fruit flavour jelly, this mango pudding uses real fruit pulp with gelatine, adding exotic mixed fruits on top to make a delicious and colourful pudding.

## Makes 1

### Ingredients
100ml evaporated milk (from tin)
100ml water
50ml mango pulp (from tin)
1½ tablespoon gelatine powder
1½ tablespoon sugar

### Garnish
3 pieces of fresh mango
3 pieces dragon fruit
3 blackberries
1 green grape

## Method
■ Warm up the water and milk to just below boiling point, dissolve the gelatine powder and sugar in the milk. Wait for the milk completely cooling down before adding the mango pulp to prevent the milk curdle. Mix the mixture well, then pour the jelly liquid into a dessert glass, cover with cling film and leave in the refrigerator to set for one hour.

■ Decorate the jelly with fresh fruits as illustrated. Cover the glass and keep in refrigerator until time to serve.

# Sweet Red Bean Soup

Sweet red bean soup is a favourite Chinese dessert, often served at the end of a dinner party to aid digestion of a heavy meal.

## Serves 3-4

### Ingredients

300g dried red bean
5g dried tangerine peel
200g rock sugar (available in all major
   Chinese supermarket)
1½ litre of water

## Method

■ Soak the dried beans and dried tangerine peel in water an hour before cooking.

■ Discard the water used for soaking the beans and tangerine peel then, using a pot with a heavy base, boil 1½ litre of water and boil the red beans until they are soft and splitting; this may take 60-90 minutes.

■ Dissolve the rock sugar in the pot. Serve the sweet red bean soup at the end of the meal.

# Red Bean Snow Balls Dessert

Red beans are widely used in Chinese cuisine for dessert; especially made into dough-like paste, in this recipe, the red bean paste is used as filling, wrapping inside a flour base meringue pastry is a modern adaptation of an old red bean buns recipe

## Makes 6

### Ingredients

4 egg white
300g ready-made red bean paste
1 tablespoon plain flour
1 tablespoon corn flour
500g Lard for fying
1 tablespoon caster sugar for dusting

## Method

- Divide the red bean paste into 6 equal parts. Roll each one into a ball and dust with plain flour.

- In an electric mixer bowl, use 4 egg whites, starting at slow speed to prevent the egg splashing. When the egg whites begin to form a thicker consistency, increase the speed and mix until they stiff and form soft peaks.

- Sift both flour and starch into the whisked egg white and mix with a slow speed until the flour and starch are completely blended into the egg white.

- Using a clean wok or large sauce pan, melt the lard and heat the oil to 180°C.

- Put the red bean paste balls into the egg and flour mixture and cover each ball evenly. Then using a large serving spoon, scoop them into the oil to fry for 1-2 minutes. The bean paste snow ball is expected to cook very rapidly.

- Remove from oil and drain off excess oil with kitchen paper towel. Before serving, sprinkle caster sugar over the snow balls.

*Useful tip:* *Although using lard for frying, the egg white and flour batter is very light, the heat from the lard hardens the batter much quicker than vegetable oil, produces a crunchy slushy coating of this dessert.*

# Tofu Pudding

One of the oldest and most popular street foods, tofu pudding originated in ancient China in the Western Han Dynasty (221-206 BC). It is made in the same way as tofu(bean curd), using soy milk that coagulated with edible calcium sulphate. The traditional way of making tofu pudding is laborious,, though nowadays, using a juice processor with soy bean grinder to extract soy milk is very easy.

## Serves 2-3

### Ingredients

500g soy bean soak in water for 11 hours
1.5 litres of water
1 tablespoon caster sugar
5g edible calcium sulphate

### Syrup

Traditionally, Chinese preferred dark cane sugar or rock sugar to make syrup.

#### DARK SYRUP

5 tablespoon muscovado sugar
100ml water

#### LIGHT SYRUP

5 tablespoon granulated sugar
100ml water

## Method

- Use a juice processor with soy bean grinder, start with small quantity of the pre-soaked soy bean and a cup of cold water to the processor, after each grinding, discard the bean residue from the filter, pour the soy milk in a heavy base pot. Continue to process small batch each time until finish.

- Use a moderate low heat to heat the soy milk until 70°C, stirring the soy milk all the time to prevent burning.

- Use a large container to dissolve the edible calcium sulphate with 3 tablespoons cold water. Pour the boiling soy milk to the container without stirring. Leave the soy milk to cool for 10 minutes, sprinkle caster sugar on top then cover it.

- Tofu pudding can be served hot or cold. Serve hot when the pudding is set,  just add your choice of syrup. If serve cold, leave the tofu pudding in the refrigerator overnight, before serving, add syrup on top.

- To prepare syrup. Boil 100ml water with 5 tablespoons sugar until dissolved.

*Useful tip:* Do not use honey as syrup to serve tofu pudding, the amino acid in honey will cause chemical changed to the tofu which likely to cause stomach upset.

水果

菜譜

# Fruit Carving and Displays

Fruit carving is an art of food presentation, an artistic creation from the professional kitchen. The art of food presentation is as important as its taste. At Chinese banquet, fruits are served to the guests at the end of the meal, an elaborate fruits presentation is a way to impress the guests, and also made them  easier for the guests to eat.

Fruit carving is by no means difficult, there are few basic techniques to follow, starting out, you can use any sharp pointed knife to practice. However, the knife must be sharp at all time to prevent bruising the fruit, always use a small whetstone for sharpening the knife.

Each kind of fruit has its own unique characteristic, professional kitchen use special carving knives set that comes with stainless steel or bronze blades. Knives with ordinary steel blades will cause discoloration of fruits.

**There are few points to remember when you are carving fruits:**

1. Choose well-formed and colourful fruits for carving, different colours and shapes offer more scope for artistic display.
2. Before carving, fruits must be washed and cleaned thoroughly.
3. Handling sharp knife, care must be exercised at all time during carving to avoid injuring yourself
4. Do not carve excessively to avoid waste and loss of nutritional value.
5. The designs should be appropriate, floral patterns are most suitable for all occasions.
6. Apples and banana should be soaked in mixture of lime juice and water before and after being carved to prevent browning.
7. Wash and dry melons and watermelons before carving.  Carve uncomplicated pattern to avoid the melon loses its natural juice, because it will lose its taste and spoil more quickly.
8. Keep each type of carved separately, store them in container with a tight lid. Keep the carved fruits refrigerated until they are ready for assemble, once assembled, serve immediately.

253

## Apple 1

1) Cut the apple in halves.
2) Remove the core
3) Cut away two thin pieces from each side of the apple in an angle to form two grooves. Discard all 4 thin pieces.
4) Turn the apple halves to have the skin-side up. Cut horizontally to 5 thick pieces.
5) Push alternate piece to form a zig zag pattern as shown.

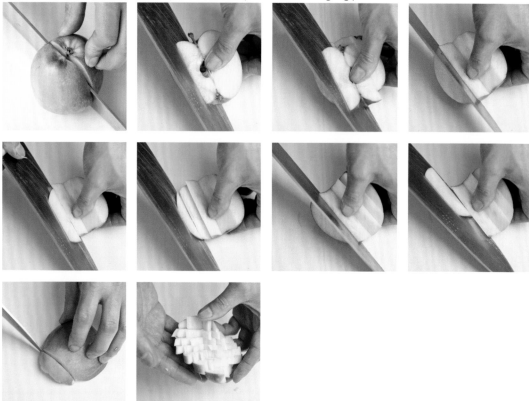

## Apple 2

1) Cut in an angle to make a small incision.
2) Cut the opposite sine also in angle to make a center piece.
3) Cut the apple the same way both sides in an angle until finish.
4) Discard the apply core.

## Apple 3

1) Cut the apple in quatres
2) Cut one side of the apple with three spikes
3) Cut the other the same
4) Score the shape of a leaf stem
5) Use the tip of the knife to remove the skin following the shape of a maple leaf

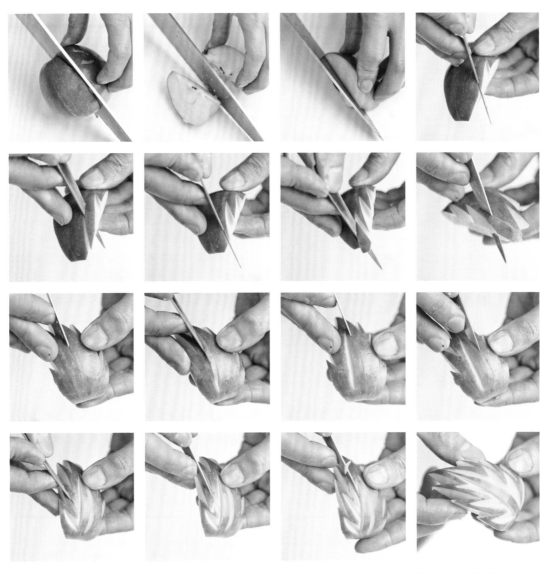

## Apple 4

1) Cut the apple in halves, then cut each half into three
2) Remove the core from each section
3) Score the apple skin with two vertical lines 2/3 down
4) Holding the apple in one side and slice the skin 2/3 down

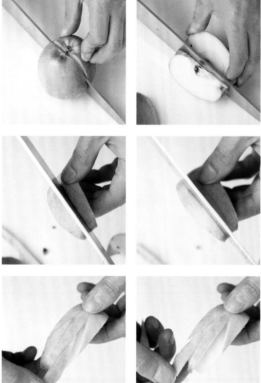

5) Cut each strip of skin in an angle half way down in an angle, so that half of the skin comes off from the cut side.

6) Soak the apple pieces in lime water before store them in a box. Cover the lid tightly and storing the apple in refrigerator.

## Grape Flower

1) Cut the top and bottom part of each grape away to form 2 flat bases.
2) Make an angle incision half way of the grape.
3) Cut the opposite angle to form a point.
4) Cut the same way until you work around the grape

5) Separating the grape by twisting the grape slightly to make the two parts come away.
6) Cut white and Red grapes to make different colours

## Melon Flower

1) Cut the melon in eight sections
2) Separating the fresh from skin all the way down to leave just the last part of each section.
3) From half way of the skin, cut a thin strip opposite to half way .
4) Cut the opposite side the same way. Bend the skin over and tuck under.

## Kiwi Fruit Flower

1) Cut the top and bottom parts of the kiwi fruit away
2) Peel the skin
3) Cut the kiwi fruit to two halves vertically.
4) Cut each half in an angle 3/4 way down.
5) Twist the halves to form the pattern

## Banana Flower

1) Cut the top and bottom parts of the banana away.
2) Use the small sharp knife to make an incision half way of the banana.
3) Work in an angle around the banana.
4) Separating the two halves
5) Peel the skin half way dow to make two banana flowers

## Mango Hedgehog

1) Cut the Mango vertically to separate the flesh from the stone in the middle.
2) Cut the opposite side. Discard the stone.
3) Score the surface of the mango flesh in an angle vertically then horizontally.
4) Push the skin of each half forward with both thumbs to form a hedgehog.

## Strawberry Flower

1) Cut the top and bottom part of each strawberry away.
2) Make an angle incision half way of the strawberry.
3) Cut the opposite angle to form a point.
4) Cut the same way until you work around the strawberry.
5) Separating the two halves by twisting the top and bottom away

## Mango Flower

This carving is only use as a decorative purpose. You will need a fruit carving knife to achieve this carving. It is best to draw the pattern on a piece of paper first as a guide to refer to.

1) Carve out five small pieces from the mango to form the middle of the flower.
2) Work in an angle to carve out a slightly larger petals around the first layer.
3) Carve the next layer of petals to form an angle.

## Melon Flower

1) Cut the melon in eight sections
2) Separating the fresh from skin from each section.
3) Cut the melon fresh in an angle to make 6 small pointed sections
4) join each section point to point to form a flower.
5) Decorate the middle with strawberry flower.

## Orange flower 1

1) Cut away the top and bottom of the orange, then cut the orange in six section.
2) Separating the skin to almost the end of the orange.
3) Cut each side of the skin in an angle to sharp thin strips.
4) Bend the cut section over and tuck under the skin to form a flower.

## Orange Flower 2

1) Cut away the top and bottom part of the orange.
2) Cut the first thin slice of the orange across, avoid cutting through the last part of the skin.
3) Cut the next slice all the way down to give a doubled slice.
4) Cut the same way for two more doubled slice. Left over the end piece uncut.

5) Open the largest slice as a base. Insert a cocktail stick through the middle.
6) Holding the end of the cocktail stick, assemble the next two layers the same way. Put a strawberry flower in the center of the top layer.
7) Insert the whole orange flower into the small half of the orange.
8) Decorate three long strips of melon skin as leaves by inserting in between the layers

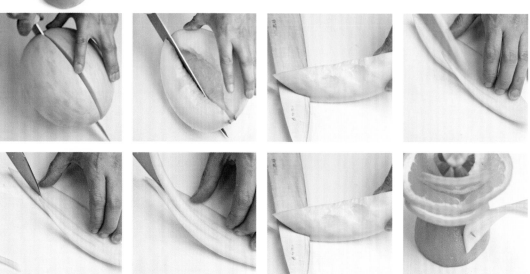

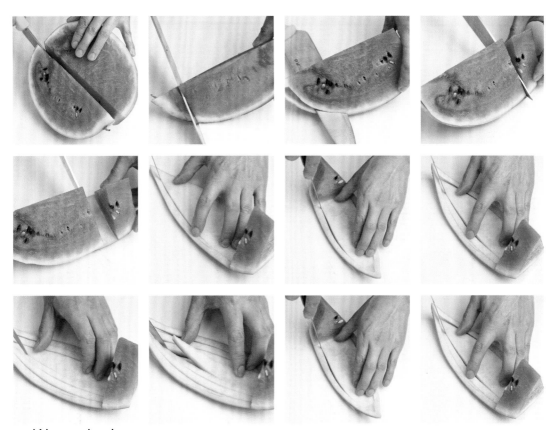

## Watermelon 1

1) Cut the water melon in two halves, and then in sections.

2) Separating the flesh and the skin to leave 4cm at the end.

3) Cut away the flesh in 4cm pieces.

4) Work on the water melon skin by cutting one side of the skin to give four long pointed angles

5) Cut the same way on the opposite side of the skin. Ensure leaving the top part uncut

6) Separating each layer by pushing each section away from each other.

7) Decorate with a grape flower on top of a strawberry flower with a cocktail stick to insert on the base.

## Watermelon 2

Same cutting as the previous pattern except cutting the watermelon skin open at the end of each layer. Using a little imagination, you can create your very own pattern with any fruit.

273

# Weights and Measures

## Volume (Dry)

| | |
|---|---|
| 1/8 teaspoon | 5 ml |
| 1/4 teaspoon | 1 ml |
| 1/2 teaspoon | 2 ml |
| 3/4 teaspoon | 4 ml |
| 1 teaspoon | 5 ml |
| 1 tablespoon | 15 ml |
| 1/4 cup | 59 ml |
| 1/3 cup | 79 ml |
| 2/3 cup | 158 ml |
| 3/4 cup | 177 ml |
| 1 cup | 225 ml |
| 2 cups or 1 pint | 450 ml |
| 3 cups | 675 ml |
| 4 cups or 1 quart | 1 litre |
| 1/2 gallon | 2 litres |
| 1 gallon | 4 litres |

## Volume (Liquid)

| | | |
|---|---|---|
| 2 tablespoons | 1 fl. oz | 30 ml |
| 1/4 cup | 2 fl. oz | 60 ml |
| 1/2 cup | 4 fl. oz | 125 ml |
| 1 cup | 12 fl. oz | 250 ml |
| 1 1/2 cup | 8 fl. oz | 375 ml |
| 2 cups or 1 pint | 16 fl. oz | 500 ml |
| 4 cups or 1 quart | 32 fl. oz | 1000 ml or 1 litre |
| 1 gallon | 128 fl. oz | 4 litres |

## Oven Temperatures

| | |
|---|---|
| 250°F | 130°C |
| 300°F | 150°C |
| 350°F | 180°C |
| 400°F | 200°C |
| 450°F | 230°C |

## Weight (Mass)

| | |
|---|---|
| 1/2 ounce | 15 grams |
| 1 ounce | 30 grams |
| 3 ounces | 85 grams |
| 3.75 ounces | 100 grams |
| 4 ounces | 115 grams |
| 8 ounces | 225 grams |
| 12 ounces | 340 grames |
| 16 ounces or 1 pound | 450 grams |

## Dry Measure Equivalents

| | | | |
|---|---|---|---|
| 3 teaspoons | 1 tsp | 1/2 ounce | 14.3g |
| 2 tablespoons | 1/8 cup | 1 ounce | 28.3g |
| 4 tablespoons | 1/4 cup | 2 ounces | 56.7g |
| 5 1/3 tablespoons | | 1/3 cup | 2.6 ounces 75.6g |
| 8 tablespoons | 1/2 cup | 4 ounces | 113.4g |
| 12 tablespoons | 3/4 cup | 6 ounces | 375g |
| 32 tablespoons | 2 cups | 16 ounces | 1 pound |

## British and American Variances

| | | | | | |
|---|---|---|---|---|---|
| cup | c., C. | usually liquid | | 237 millilitres | 16 tablespoons or 8 ozs |
| ounce | fl oz, fl. oz. | American | liquid | 29.57 millilitres | |
| | | British | either | 28.41 millilitres | |
| gallon | gal. | American | liquid | 3.785 litres | 4 quarts |
| | | British | either | 4.546 litres | 4 quarts |
| inch | in; in. | | | | 2.54 centimetres |
| ounce | foz, oz. | American | dry | 28.35 grams | 1/16 pound |
| | | | either | see OUNCE | see OUNCE |
| pint | p., pt. | American | liquid | 0.473 litre | 1/8 gallon or 16 ozs |
| | | | dry | 0.551 litre | 1/2 quart |
| | | British | either | 0.568 litre | |
| pound | lb. | British | dry | 453.592 grams | 16 ounces |
| quart | q., qt. | American | liquid | 0.946 litre | 1/4 gallon or 32 ozs |
| | | American | dry | 1.101 litres | 2 pints |
| | | British | either | 1.136 litres | |
| teaspoon | t., tsp., tsp. | British | either | about 5 ml | 1/3 tablespoon |
| tablespoon | t., tbs., tbsp. | British | either | about 15 ml | 3 teaspoons or 1/2 ozs |

# Recipe index

Page numbers in **Bold** refer to illustrations.

# Recipe index

# Acknowledgements

Writing a cookbook is one of my ambition since the day I started to
work in the kitchen when I was 15 years old.
During the preparation of this book, I am grateful to so many people,
who have given me their guidance and generous ideas.
My staff at my restaurants, office and friends who worked tirelessly to
make this book possible.

I am extremely thankful to my wife and partner Dorian for her
patience, forbearance and her attention to detail.
Under her supervision and the photographer Xunbo Tang,
they brought out the taste, the aroma and the beauty of all the dishes
through all the images featured in this cookbook.

I would like to extend my thanks to Kathy Cheng, who worked on both
English and Chinese versions of this cookbook tirelessly
behind the scenes, providing her knowledge of food history.
Testing each recipe's weights, measure and making method.

My staff Derek Liang, researched relevant information to make
publishing this book in reality.

Finally, My chefs at Wing Wah restaurant,
Guoming Liu, Mingkui Chen, Jianrong Li and Wutao Dai.
Their determination to use the same principles and standard,
cooking the best food to serve customers in all our restaurants.

BONG LAM Cookbook